Kaleidoscope

Kaleidoscope

TRISCH ROSEMA

BALBOA.
PRESS

A DIVISION OF HAY HOUSE

Balboa Press books may be ordered through booksellers or by contacting:

Balboa Press
A Division of Hay House
1663 Liberty Drive
Bloomington, IN 47403
www.balboapress.com
1-(877) 407-4847

Because of the dynamic nature of the Internet, any web addresses or links contained in
this book may have changed since publication and may no longer be valid. The views
expressed in this work are solely those of the author and do not necessarily reflect the
views of the publisher, and the publisher hereby disclaims any responsibility for them.

The author of this book does not dispense medical advice or prescribe the use
of any technique as a form of treatment for physical, emotional, or medical
problems without the advice of a physician, either directly or indirectly. The
intent of the author is only to offer information of a general nature to help you
in your quest for emotional and spiritual well-being. In the event you use any
of the information in this book for yourself, which is your constitutional right,
the author and the publisher assume no responsibility for your actions.

Any people depicted in stock imagery provided by Thinkstock are models,
and such images are being used for illustrative purposes only.
Certain stock imagery © Thinkstock.

Printed in the United States of America

ISBN: 978-1-4525-6796-9 (sc)
ISBN: 978-1-4525-6798-3 (hc)
ISBN: 978-1-4525-6797-6 (e)

Library of Congress Control Number: 2013902103

Balboa Press rev. date: 3/13/2013

IN A MYRIAD OF COLOURS, EACH
INDIVIDUAL PIECE FALLS PERFECTLY INTO
PLACE, CREATING A MASTERPIECE

"Every worthwhile accomplishment, big or little, has its stages of drudgery and triumph; a beginning, a struggle and a victory."

—Mahatma Gandhi

This book is for my children, without whom my life would not have been as colourful as it has been.

It is also for Peter, my adoring husband who always believes in me, no matter what. He is publishing his first novel alongside me. Here's to your great success, my darling!

Contents

Vibrant, Dazzling, Colourful Kaleidoscopes

Why Kaleidoscope?

I n my childhood, kaleidoscopes were given to kids with ADD (Attention Deficit Disorder) to keep them from bouncing off the walls. None of today's killer drug stuff went into our bodies back then. Not that ADD was even diagnosed in those early 1960's, I don't think. We were just considered 'difficult' children who demanded attention and needed a bloody good hiding to sort us out.

Clearly I was one of those children.

I had many kaleidoscopes. Some I'd bought with pocket money, others were gifts for birthdays and Christmases.

I would lie on the soft green lawn outside the front of our house, twisting the outer flange, backwards and forwards, marvelling at the patterns I could make, spending hours enthralled by this magical tube. Each pattern was different to the next. None were even slightly the same as the ones preceding them. Colours flashed by in a haze of beautiful hues and patterns fell into place just perfectly.

These colours stilled my soul; they transported me to a place of beauty and magic, where anything was possible. A place where my imagination could run riot, an imagination I did not share for fear I would be labelled uncontrollable. I would see pictures and make up stories to go with those patterns and colours and I would hug this secret to myself, guarding it jealously, lying quietly on that beautiful green lawn, pointing my kaleidoscope towards the light of the blue sky on a perfect South African summer's day.

Possibly, this is where my love of colour came from.

PREFACE

9 JUNE 2012

I've joined a book writing group. I must be mad. What has possessed me to even think I could possibly do this? I have spent the past five days plotting and planning and confusing myself six ways from Sunday (I rested on the seventh). Yip *le book* aka *the novel inside of me* just gets bigger and bigger and I can't remember who's who in the zoo.

Michelle, our group organizer, has suggested I mind-map this. I've realized mind mapping is for other people. I can't do them. They go all over the place and the connectors end up looking like a huge pot of over-cooked spaghetti. Actually, today I have mashed potatoes for brains. Make some gravy to go with it and we have the stirrings (pardon the pun) of a good tagine. Or stew. Depending on what you want to call it.

So I've scrapped the idea of *the novel that's inside of me* for when I'm more confident about writing a believable one, and instead I am going back to writing how I write. In the first person, ahem, like me. Like as I speak. I can write about me, as me. And if anyone thinks I am rather immodest, they're welcome to think what they will, but I do hope they enjoy reading about the colours which have made up my technicolor life so far.

Oh my, who wants to read about me? I wonder in the middle of the night. I've woken up sweating despite the minus 3 degree Highveld winter. I admit the sweating is actually the big M. That condition we fifty-something women all whisper about and pretend we are immune to. You know, like when you get to my age you're supposed to go through this life-changing experience that is rumoured to be the second coming of age? Which, in actual fact, is bullshit? It renders you forgetful and miserable. It puffs you up, gets you all puce pink and glowing and your poor husband, kids, dogs, cats and koi fish all hide away and pray you'll go for HRT. Fast.

Well, I reckon, maybe my kids will enjoy reading about me. After all, I have a vague idea of what my own parents were like, where they came from, how they loved, lived, played. They were old when I was born. I remember my friends always asking why my granny was bringing me to school. I hope my children will never think that of me. I want them to remember me as *'oh crap, there she goes again'* when my mind is addled, my bladder is weak and I'm being kept alive on as many drugs per day as a Smartie box has Smarties in it. Yeah!

So, I did do a sort of a mind mapping thing in my *mal de mer* state in the middle of the night. I sat up, grabbed a box of tissues, wiped the sweat from my brow and then, pulling my iPad across my lap, I started to type.

The cats gave me a seriously disdainful look, as only cats know how to do. Tucking their heads back up their bums, shielding their eyes from the light with their tails, they cuddled up once again between my knees. Which, if you must know, were spread apart in a very, very unladylike fashion. But we do what we must for the kitties. We spread our legs.

Peter, the man of my life, my soul-mate, my partner, my knight in shining armour, my lover and best friend... can you hear the violins playing in the background?... well, he just snorted, turned over, put his back to the light (and me), and proceeded to go back to la-la land and sweet dreams of who knows what.

But I swear, if he dreams of his high school wet dream (who has turned out to be the most wonderful woman and I love her to bits) just one more time, I'm going to give him a seriously big fat *klap*!

I have used some artistic licence in my story, perhaps to give it a little more flavour, perhaps because that's how it was. But throughout, I have endeavoured to keep the identities of my friends and family (unless they're dead and long gone or they have agreed to me publishing their names) safe by altering some details here and there. If ever they get to read this book, I am sure they will recognise themselves and I thank them in advance for contributing to the success of this memoir.

And with that artistic licence comes my take on all things good, and bad. They are merely my own observations and opinions. There is no need to start a FaceBook group to boycott my ramblings –nothing I write is politically motivated or meant to start World War III and there is without doubt no intentional harm meant to any person, any dog, cat, horse, bird, koi fish or otherwise.

I must at this point also thank a few other people.

To my special friend, Cynthia Daniels who facilitated the publishing of my memoir, thank you. Without your persuasive powers, I probably would have left it in cyberspace. I owe you the first hard copy, my friend—signed *nogal!*

Michelle Ainslee. Thank you for putting our writing group together and encouraging us each step of the way. Peter, Su-Mari, Conny, Antoinette and Jill, Pieter and the other Michelle, inspired writers in the group who too are publishing their books—well done and good luck. I wish you great success. And Pieter, thank you for suggesting that each chapter is represented by a colour. That's exactly how each chapter of my life has been so far—colourful!

And then, of course, thanks to myself... just kidding!

It's not all Black and White

The ambulance men stumbled down the gangplank, I'm told, carrying a stocky forty-two year old woman off the HMS Carnarvon Castle on a khaki green canvas stretcher. The ship, which had the distinction of being the first twin-screwed motor vessel of the Union Castle Ships, had berthed in Cape Town just as my mother started birthing me.

They rushed her, heaving in extreme pain, and in the throes of a placental abruption, to the Peninsula Maternity Home in District Six, Cape Town. The area was, in those days, where freed slaves, labourers, immigrants and Jews lived in a vibrant community near the port. I can just hear my Grandmother turning in her grave, complaining about those immigrants and Jews. She was terribly anti-Semitic. As were many South Africans during those post-war years.

I was delivered by caesarean section three months prematurely. I'm told they dumped me, quite unceremoniously, into a kidney bowl while the doctors fought to save my mother's life. A placental abruption, depending on the severity, can have serious effects on both mother and foetus. I say foetus, because at 29 weeks, and weighing in under two pounds, I really believe the medical staff would have taken one look at me and decided there was no way I could survive.

But, being a feisty thing, I took a rather scrawny breath into my under-developed lungs and gave such a howl there was no mistaking that I was alive, thank you very much. Knowing myself, I am sure I would have been rather indignant at being left in a silver bowl and ignored quite like that.

I find this ironic, because I was born with the proverbial silver spoon in my mouth. As I've aged, however, I've stopped getting quite so prickly about being abandoned in the kidney bowl. I've come to the realization that I actually enjoy all things silver. Silver earrings, silver goblets, silver salvers, silver sandals, you name it, if it's blingy and its silver, or even better, platinum (which looks like silver too but oh, so much more expensive), I love it.

I was born in the apartheid era of South Africa, where white was white and black was not black. It was brown, or rather, various shades and hues of brown.

There were brown black people, sometimes referred to as natives, other times referred to as Bantu, but mostly people called them *kaffirs* which as we all know is a seriously derogatory and politically incorrect word which we best don't even utter these days in our rainbow nation. But that is what they were called back then and sadly, many accepted it.

In South Africa, there are nine different black nations, or ethnic groups, the largest of which are the Zulu people. Each group has their own language (which now makes up South Africa's official languages) and culture.

Our late housekeeper, Sarah, was a gentle Xhosa woman. Her

skin was the color of highly polished mahogany. It was smooth and plump, not a wrinkle to be found. She was extremely neat and proud. It showed in the way she wore her colourful headdress and skirts, decorated with black binding. Sarah was our mother. After the death of her husband and then a couple of years later, her only daughter, Sarah arrived on our doorstep one morning with a chubby baby boy who she had named Gift. She had adopted him from her local Welfare Society.

"Ta!" Gift was clever. He would spot my husband Peter across the room and he'd run towards the cupboard, pointing to where the marshmallows were kept.

"Say please?" Peter would prompt him.

"Ta, Peta, ta," the little guy would ask, his toothless grin melting Peter's heart. He would be rewarded with two marshmallows. One white, one pink. Little Gift would shove them in his mouth, chewing away on his gums, dribble running down his burnished brown fat little chin.

Our mother died last year. She was riddled with ovarian cancer. By the time we knew she was sick, it was too late. We miss her terribly.

Little Gift is well looked after. Sarah made sure of that. Unfortunately, we have lost contact with him because his family don't trust us the same way Sarah did.

That is the way of the many cultures that make up our country. Each one is distrustful of the next. Sad.

⁓

There were brown Indian people - not to be confused with the Red Indian people of the Americas who lived in tepee's and had weird names like Running Wolf and Man Who Sit With Hot Rock on Head. The South African Indians in those early nineteen hundreds came from, well, India. They were originally brought in to our country as slaves on the trade ships and most were (and still are) to be found around the sea port city of Durban. Some Indians were quite black actually, depending on which part of India their ancestors came from. Others were a beautiful bronzed colour, reminiscent of the Bodhi tree under which Buddha found enlightenment. But the one thing they all had in common, and still have to this day, is an accent that is entirely their own. When speaking English, an Indian's 'double you' becomes a 'we', everything is 'so much of' and no matter if they now live in Perth or Pretoria, Dresden or Dubai, Indians the world over speak English with the exact same accent. Go figure.

"Ey man, Petah," said our friend Dyah, a Tamil-speaking Indian of Southern Indian ancestry who had a deep almost-black skin, "you gotting a mean matcheen there, man. It looks so much of sexy!" This was when we stopped in to see Dyah in the Indian community of Shallcross, Durban. Peter, my then-boyfriend slash significant-other, now husband, had just bought a very cute little white Mazda Miata and we were, roof-down, zooming along the coastline to the Wild Coast to indulge in a weekend of pleasure. Like gambling, sex and sun. Oh alright, forget the sun, it's bad for our white skins anyway.

Dyah was engaged to a wonderful lady of maharajah, or royal, descent. She was a professor of law, specialising in gender justice, amongst other subjects. Now her skin was that of golden honey and her features were more refined, reminding me of the photographs of Indian Maharani's in their beautifully embroidered and embellished sari's during the British colonial period. This brought me to the question of how did one best describe South African Indians?

While American Indians were 'red', I did a bit of dipstick research with my friends and came to the conclusion that South African Indians ranged from brown to black, from orange to white. Some were even yellow. Depending on what part of India they came from originally.

South African Indians are family oriented. They all live together. Usually happily. They wear Prada and Guess, Nike and Gap. They drive cars with over-spec'd sound systems and shadow-line tyres. They hang out at places like Gateway and Sun City. And they love Bollywood movies with music tracks, choreography, colourful gilded costumes and romantic love themes.

So where was our black and white only apartheid South Africa back then when I was born in District Six?

Continuing on with the brown theme of black in this rainbow nation, I remembered there were Cape Malay brown people too.

The terms Malay and Muslim are often used as synonyms but strictly speaking, Malay stands for that section of the local Muslim community in which the descendants of Eastern Malays are to be found. They were considered respectable folk who worked hard and did not drink.

Food is an important part of Malay life and Malay women can cook. Using exotic spices such as tamarind for crayfish curry, cloves and cinnamon in their *denningvleis* lamb dishes, to syrupy *koeksusters* which are still eaten at tea-times and which have become a national favourite. Oh, and the Malay Mama's can cook a mean *bobotie*.

Malay mothers are also very good at crocheting doilies. Go into any Malay home and you'll find doilies everywhere. They line the back of couches and chairs to prevent *Brylcreemed* hair staining the velveteen cushions of the settee's they purchased from *Morkels, your two-year guarantee store*. Doilies are found on side tables and dressers, the dining room boasts one long doily running the length of the table too, typically with a plastic pot plant plonked dead centre on top of it. On the back of the toilet cistern is usually to be found, and in shades to suit the colour scheme of the bathroom, a Barbie doll complete with crocheted doily dress which hides a spare loo roll. Oh hell man, the Malay men even wear doilies on their heads. Why? Coz their Malay mothers said so.

Now there were brown Coloured people too, not to be confused with the Malays. While both groups were Afrikaans speaking, Malays generally followed the Islamic faith while Coloureds followed the Dutch Reformed Christian faith. Coloureds were really a mish-mash with their genes going way back into the past with Khoisan and Bushman ancestry and perhaps a bit of Bantu and European lineage thrown in just for good measure.

You will find Cape Coloureds most often running around with no front teeth shouting profanities like *jou ma se moer* while swigging on the obligatory Friday afternoon bottle of *kak bek* and leering at all the young *cherries* while slowly getting more and more *dronk vir driet*.

Cape Coloureds are a breed apart. They also have the most delightful sense of humour.

Some years ago I was driving two coloured ladies who worked for me to their homes late afternoon. Both had just recently married and they were comparing notes on the ins and outs of suddenly finding themselves responsible for keeping their men happy. And as all women know, that means feeding them. Both women were complaining that they'd picked up weight since being newly-wed as they now were expected to cook a full meal each night when they got home from work.

Of course this all took place in a wonderful English/Afrikaans that only the Coloured people know how to speak. Sorta like Kitchen Dutch. It went something like this:

"Ag, tjy weet, Tjarmie, tjus tha otha day I hed to buy new *pee-tsama's* kors tha ones mah mutha did buy me for tha *wittebrood* dusn't fit no more," she lamented. (*Oh, you know, Charmie, just the other day I had to buy new pyjamas because the ones my mother bought me for my honeymoon don't fit any more.*)

Charmolene answered from the back of the car, "Tsa, I know for whatchoo say, Priscilla. Ik het ook fet opgetel since tha wedding. Las' night I got on the scale in tha bathroom and it read 'to be continued'." (*Yes, I know what you're saying Priscilla. I've picked up weight since the wedding too.*)

❧

Then there were us Whites, or as we were still called in the sixties, Europeans.

After Jan van Riebeeck had landed in the Cape in 1652 to set up the Fort of Good Hope as a so-called refreshment station for the Dutch East India Company, the British, the French and any other pilgrim who wished to, set sail for the Cape and settled into their new homeland.

My paternal great-grandfather, Berend Blomkamp, did just that. He secured a piece of land to farm, worked out he was a mason and not a grape farmer, sold the land and moved into the *dorp*. Then he sailed back to Holland and found himself a wife. This was a necessity as he didn't have a clue how to look after himself in the Kaapse Goede Hoop. While in Holland, though, my great-grandmother found she was expecting and so Frederick Benjamin was born there. They joined Berend when Frederick was old enough to sail back to the Cape. Frederick enjoyed his youth. Being the only child of the union, he was limp-wristed and spoilt. His every whim was pandered to by his doting mother.

Eventually he was sent off university (by his father) where he graduated with a degree in Architecture and a socialite wife whom he had picked up somewhere along the way.

Bless her heart; one of the Europeans living in Cape Town in the sixties was my Grandmother. She was a lady. A whitest of white, palest of pale, peachiest of peachy complexions, British lady. I believe my grandmother just could not imagine her granddaughter being born any place like District Six. Because, as the Mayoress of Cape Town (that's only because my Grandfather was the Mayor you understand), well, what on the Good Lords Earth would people think of that?

Let me tell you about Alma Charlotte, my Grandmother.

She was a Jupp you understand. And Jupps were toffs. They originated from Sussex, England, with a smidgeon of a hint of an aristocratic background. The Cape Jupps thought of themselves as landed gentry.

As one of the upper class, Alma Charlotte would never have been seen dead without her stockings. Or her teeth. She was a diminutive figure with peroxided and permed hair which was set at the local hairdresser every Friday morning where she had a standing appointment. They would wash and condition her locks and then, using pink jelly-like Dippity Doo, the hairdresser would set her fair hair in green rollers, finishing it off with a blue net which would protect her hair from flying up into the heated elements of the wall-mounted hairdryers under which my grandmother and a couple of other socialites would sit, knees together, ankles crossed, handbags at their feet, reading the latest copy of Town and Country.

My grandmother wore twin sets and pearls and never went anywhere without a lace edged hanky tucked into the sleeve of her cardigan at her wrist. She walked upright with her shoulders pulled back which proudly displayed her cross-your-heart-bra separated breasts. I suspect she wore a girdle too as she had a fairly small waist. Clearly a gene I did not inherit from that side of the family.

Grandmother (I was never allowed to call her Granny or Grandma or Nanna), well, Grandmother spent her days socialising. She played bridge and bowls (never together of course) and at 4pm each day she would have a little tipple. A Ginger Square to be exact.

Grandmother would sit in the drawing room—lord, yes, it wasn't a lounge, I beg you—and as the carriage clock chimed its Westminster full hour permutation in E major, she would slowly sip her Ginger Square from a beautiful Baccarat tumbler. The Westminster's chime is traditionally, though without substantiation, believed to be a set of variations on the four notes that make up the fifth and sixth measures of 'I know that my Redeemer Liveth' from Handel's Messiah. And after her tipple each day at 4pm, I am certain Grandmother livethed.

She also had this weird thing she did when she went to the loo. She'd spend a penny. I never quite understood what she was spending her pennies on in there and anyway, South Africa had already converted to Rands and Cents. Didn't Granny, er, Grandmother, know that? I wasn't about to tell her. There are some secrets you just don't share with a Grandmother.

⌒

Those pennies eventually were converted into Rands and Cents. I was given 10c pocket money every Saturday. I spent that 10c every Saturday too, never saving a penny. Well, there weren't any more of those left anyway coz Grandmother was spending them, so what the hell.

Saturdays were 'we're-going-to-town' days. My father would park his fire-engine red Renault Dauphin on the Foreshore. We would traipse up Adderley Street, me hanging onto my mother's hand, hoppity skipping in excitement. My 10c would be burning a hole in my pocket, enticing thoughts of what I would be spending it on swirling around in my head.

First stop was the butchery in Long Street. My mother would lean over the butchers block, choosing the best cuts of meat, ordering a pound of this, half a pound of that. Then the meat would be wrapped up in heavy-weight, unwaxed brown paper and loaded into a bag, ready to be delivered. In his navy and white striped butcher's apron, Meneer van Rensburg would reach over the counter and hold out a fat juicy red Vienna sausage to me, both ends twisted and knotted, the skin so tight, its innards nearly bursting out.

"*Dankie Meneer*," I'd say in my best Afrikaans accent, while simultaneously shoving the delicious treat into my mouth. I so looked forward to those sossies on Saturdays.

While Mom and I were at the butcher, Dad would be doing the family's banking at the Standard Bank of South Africa. He would wait on the steps of the bank for Mom and I as we walked back down Adderley Street. The three of us would then stop in at the CNA (Central News Agency) where Dad would browse the magazine section, paging through the flying magazines, while Mom collected her standing order of The Woman's Weekly. It would be rolled up and secured with a length of cash register paper torn off the roll and stuck down with a bit of sticky tape. Moms name would be written in neat upper case block lettering with a black ink pen on the piece of white till roll paper. Sometimes the ink would stain my mother's gloves and she would bitch and complain that it would never come out. But every Saturday I would notice while holding her hand, hoppity skipping up Adderley Street toward the butchery, that her white gloves were white as white could be. I believe it had something to do with blue soap.

Finally, we'd get out of the CNA and make our way to the OK Bazaars—the first store ever to have moving stairs. I would jump on the escalator with all the confidence in the world that I wouldn't fall off, despite my heart hammering in my bony chest and my hands getting all clammy and my knees going all wobbly. But ride them stairs I would, every Saturday, come South-Easter or not. Up and down, up and down, while Mom was scouring the wool department for just the right shade of grey to knit Dad another cable cardigan.

Eventually my mother would make her way downstairs to the supermarket, leaving my poor Father to oversee the spend of my pocket money in the toy department. I am certain that I got far more than my 10c would ever pay for, as I not only went home laden with little Addis pots and pans (was that a sign I would one day enjoy cooking?) but I'd also have at least 1c in change. Which I'd spend on Tiger toffees and Wilson's caramel squares at the corner café near our house.

And on the Saturdays that the infamous south-easter wind was blowing, and the clouds were rolling in over Table Mountain, I would lie on the back seat of Dad's car and be lulled to sleep while on our way home to our little white house with a wire fence and a rockery filled with cactuses, er cactusis, er cacti, which my mom would water every other evening while chatting over the fence to Mrs Wilkins, the neighbour from number 21.

ROSES ARE RED, VIOLETS ARE BLUE, CACTI ARE GREEN AND THEIR THORNS *EINA* YOU!

Anyone worth their salt (and a slice of lemon) will know that tequila comes from the cactus plant. Actually, to be correct, from the blue agave plant. This, while it has a really fancy name, is actually just a good old cactus-looking succulent which grows in the desert near Tequila (duh) in one of the provinces of Mexico.

The red volcanic soil in that part of the world is nothing like my mother's rockery which was being watered the day I had my first experience with a cactus plant. Succulent or not, tequila or not, I got prickled big time.

Now all little 4-year old girls have visions of becoming prima ballerina's—don't they? Most do. I didn't. Most of the time I wanted to be just like Stirring Moth.

"Stirring who?" my doting father asked me as I raced down the driveway, red plastic helmet on head, skinny little legs peddling my blue tin car with a large white No. 5 decal stuck on the front bonnet, just over the yellow GT stripe.

"Daddy! You know who Stirring Moth is, you're just teasing me." I said, exasperatedly, rolling my eyes heavenwards and letting out a loud sigh. Often this would be accompanied by both hands being placed on hips, and one foot tapping a show of impatience.

"Daddy, you know, the racing driver we saw at the bioscope when Alma went to see Elvis Presley."

I fondly remember my father having a good chuckle at how I referred to Sir Stirling Moss OBE. We had watched a segment about him on S.A. News Reel just before the main feature was about to start. His racing career had ignited a fire in my little belly, fuelling (pun intended) visions of racing around Silverstone in my little blue tin car. Stirring Moth was my first hero.

But that particular day in 1965 while Mom and Mrs Wilkins were yakking over the fence, the cacti in the rockery being splashed with cool water, Stirring Moth had been overshadowed by images of Odette/Odile in Swan Lake. Just that morning my ballet teacher had shown her class of aspiring little ballerina's photographs of Margot Fonteyn and Rudolph Nureyev in a *pas de deux* from Swan Lake. She had played us a scratched vinyl of Tchaikovsky's Opus 20 on the new turntable which was set up in the corner of the studio.

I could hear the music, the haunting sounds of the clarinet and oboes, rising up to the crescendo of the drums and brass instruments interspersed with the sound of the water from the hosepipe (which made me want to wee), inspiring me as I jete'd from rock to rock in my white cotton summer dress with the pink ribbons at the shoulders.

"Patricia!" my mother admonished me. She only ever used my full name if I was causing trouble and/or if I was in trouble. If she used all my given names, then I knew things had become extremely serious and best I stop otherwise I'd get a good backhander for sure.

"Patricia, will you stop that right now!" she cried, "you're going to slip and hurt yourself."

Of course, all 4-year old aspiring ballerinas would think the old duck had lost her marbles. I was sure of foot; I was light and flighty, elegant and swan-like. Until I did a swan-like duck right into a cactus plant. Bum first.

I swear my mother put those words out into the universe on purpose and that's why I ended up on my stomach with the doctor pulling cactus thorns out of my rear end with a pair of tweezers. Each single thorn removal was painful. With every hook hanging on tight inside my cute little rump and saying 'na-ah I'm stuck fast here and you ain't getting me out that easily' I cried as they were forcibly pulled out of my petite rear end.

I spent days lying in bed on my stomach. I could not sit for weeks. I cried when I was put into the bath. The hot water stung my already dented derriere.

And that cactus certainly put paid to my visions of ever performing the *vrekking* duck scene from Swan Lake with the Bolshoi Ballet.

Some forty-six years later, I would once again experience the pain of the cactus plant.

"Happy Birthday to you!" sang friends at a surprise 50th birthday party thrown for me at one of my favourite restaurants.

The restaurant specialized in Mozambican food, from *prawns nacionale* to the best peri-peri chicken this side of the *boerewors* curtain. I was not only delighted at going to O'Petisco for my favourite meal, but I was also delightfully surprised to see all my friends there that evening. I love a party.

It started with a very gentle little back-hander called a Jagermeister. You either love 'em or you hate 'em. I love them. So

I had one. Then I had two and then three. My margarita-drinking pal, Diana, lined up the tequila's. One for her, two for me. One for her, three for me. One for me, six for her. She had to catch up. Between eating buttery-rich deep pink prawns with my fingers, the juices running down my arms, drinking tequilas and shoving decadently rich chocolate cake into my mouth, I also got stuck into my newest favourite drink which Diana introduced me to. Patron. The coffee one. Yum.

My DH was my DD that night. He had to be. His neurologist had discharged him from hospital that day (unbeknown to me especially for the surprise dinner he had arranged from his hospital bed). She had given him strict instructions not to touch a drop of alcohol and to report back to the hospital the following Monday morning.

At 6pm, I was about to start making supper.

"Let's go out for dinner," Peter suggested, "I'm sick of hospital food."

It sounded like a fine idea to me. I wasn't really in the mood to start cooking anyway, having spent the last two weeks running up and down from the hospital. I was exhausted. An evening out where someone else did the cooking would be a blessing.

Which is how Peter got me to the restaurant without me even catching on that something was up.

The restaurant was decorated with banners proclaiming me to now be 50 years old. Did that mean I had to suddenly become an adult? I downed another Patron. Did that mean I had to now take responsibility for my actions? Diana passed me another shot glass and I downed that one too, and then three and then another four.

By the time we were on the way home, we (I know for sure that means Diana and I) were thoroughly sozzled. Fortunately it was the weekend and we didn't have to work the next day.

Now, whether I'm sozzled or not, I still remember to take my make-up off before I go to bed. Brushing my teeth is another story however... the thought of putting a toothbrush near my soft-palate while I'm pickled does not bode well.

But that night, I got into the shower. I remember this. I remember using my favourite Fenjal soap in the shower. I remember reaching out for my lovely fluffy white towel when I stepped out of the shower.

And then the world went blank. It also went 'hello, that's a nice carpet I think I'll sleep on it'.

Which is where Peter found me a little while later.

It took some years for the man of my life to find me. Frankly, I found him.

I'd been working as a travelling sales person (oh dearie me, wrong profession for me to be in) and after numerous cold calls which were not producing any future revenue, I got through to a very nice sounding man called Manfred who said 'call me again next week'. So I did, and he'd say, "I'm really busy now, call me again next week'. Which is exactly what I would do. I am really good at following orders, so I would pencil into my diary (this in the days before Outlook Calendar) 'phone Manfred' in the To Do column of my A4 Executive Diary, and religiously I would phone him on said day. And so I'd be pencilling in again 'phone Manfred' because he would say "I'm just so snowed under right now, phone me again next week."

Being the fox-terrier I am, I got my teeth in and I did not let go. Manfred did. Well, he gave in. Eventually. I had an appointment to meet with him.

I got to his office only to hear, "I'm running late because I'm so busy so I'll have to see you another time."

Was I surprised? Hell, no. But then he did the nicest thing anyone would ever do for me. He led me down a very long corridor into the office of the most gorgeous looking guy I'd ever seen in my life... and who I disliked intensely at first sight.

You're confused right? Wrong. Manfred introduced me to the man of my dreams, the man who would become my best friend, my lover, my husband, the father of all our children, our cats and dogs, two parakeets, twenty-one koi fish and a hedgehog named Rachmaninoff.

But that didn't detract from the fact that when I first met him I thought (even though he was so drop-dead gorgeous) that he was the most irritating, arrogant, rude, did I mention drop-dead gorgeous, son-of-a-bitch.

There's that special moment in your life when, without even understanding what the universe is up to, you just *know* that the person in front of you is going to be the most important being in your life. That's how I felt when I met Peter. We clicked on some cosmic level which, in those miserable years of my life, I sorely needed.

That day, while I was standing in Peter's office, prickling and getting all hot and flushed at the same time, my heartbeat sounding in my ears, the angels in heaven smiled down, nodding and fluffing their wings and proclaiming "at long last... Hallelujah!"

At this point I could just hear those harps being fined tuned, arpeggio's running up and down the strings. The trumpets were trumpeting and the celestial cymbals were clashing. As were we.

"Well, if you can do this better than me, why the bloody hell don't you just do it and save yourselves a lot of money?"

I stormed out of his office and straight back into Manfred's, past a bemused and dishevelled secretary. I'm sure Manfred had just shagged her in the rest-rooms. So that's what he was so busy doing that he couldn't meet with me. He was a dog, but a very nice dog who would become a great friend to us through the years. I plonked myself down in the visitors chair opposite him.

"He's a nice guy, Trisch," he placated, "he's just a really clever guy who's not used to clever woman coming in and knowing what they're talking about. Oh, and he's just trying to impress you too."

"Hell of a way to do so!" I exclaimed.

But he did impress me. Especially when he phoned to say he was in the reception area of the company I was working for and could I please come out of my hiding place and talk to him. I did, rather gingerly, making sure there were no runs in my pantyhose and that my hair was in place and my lipstick was not smudged.

Fast forward six hours.

The Sunnyside Park Hotel was notorious for its Friday afternoon 'yay-its-the-weekend' party crowds. 4pm on a Friday and every worker-bee from Braamfontein to Benoni flocked to the Sunnyside to bring in the weekend. Booze flowed freely, some people clutched ice-cold bottles of beer, others indulged in white wine spritzers. Women primped and pouted in their power suits, with wide belts and broad shouldered jackets. It was the eighties. Gin-swilling Sue Ellen Ewing in the TV series Dallas, had brought shoulder pads into fashion. South African women went mad. You were not dressed unless your shoulders were reminiscent of a player getting into gear for the Superbowl. Men in suits with labels like Carducci and St. Laurent, wearing red ties and super-shiny shoes leeched around, spotting who was good for a pickup. Lecherous bums.

That Friday, Peter and I shared a bottle of really, really, but I mean, *really* good red wine and then, we did some seriously really, really, I really mean *really*, good snogging in his car. In the parking lot of the Sunnyside Park Hotel under the century old oak trees.

After which there were some runs in my pantyhose, my hair was very definitely out of place and my lipstick… what lipstick?

Vodka plus a Red Bull
equals All Fall Down

Peter failed ski school. He was expelled after three hours. I'm not sure if it was because he just cannot ski, or if he was clever enough to get out of the physical exertion of learning to climb up the mountain on day one. Question. Why would they teach you to climb up a mountain anyway? Isn't the idea of skiing to get down as fast as you possibly can? I thought so.

So anyway, there we are, Peter, myself and two of our four children, standing on the side of the slopes of an ominous mountain peak called Zwolfer. We're in matching-smatching ski jackets. You can't lose each other. If you do, you just point to yourself and say 'he's wearing this in'—and you mention the colour. Peter is decked out in his trademark Coca-Cola red, Dane wears safe navy blue, Justyn's green jacket reminds me of Hyperama Heydays and my jacket is the brightest of bright, a canary-has-nothing-on-it yellow. Or as Gregory, our youngest little shit, would say, hello! Which is about what I was asking myself as I peered over the edge of the red run.

"Hello, self. Are you nuts? Bananas? Banana-split nuts with ice-cream on the top mad? You must be. You're going to break your neck if you think you're going to get down this mountain in one piece."

But let me side-track a moment here and go back to the nursery slope ski-school days of Saalbach, Austria. It's four o'clock. The last ski lift is taking us to the top of the nursery slopes. Peter has already fallen off his skis once. Dane is trying to help get him back upright, steady on his feet and stable enough to just hang onto the T-bar for the next 50 metres. Oops, man down again. Dane picks him up, the operator stops the T-bar, and someone shouts "Achtung! Let's Go!" Dane responds *"achtung se moer"* while Peter gingerly wobbles onto all fours, his knees and hands trying to dig into the soft snow to stop him from sliding right back down to where he started from. Then, pulling himself up along Dane's length, he manages to get onto his feet. Dane retrieves the skis and helps to lock Peter back in. I've continued up to the top to the Hinterhag Alm pretending I really don't know these people, I just happen to be wearing the same make of jacket; just in a different colour by pure coincidence.

Justyn is, as usual, MIA.

The Hinterhag Alm is alive with the sounds of Austrian and Tirolean music. On a very small stage in the centre of the oak panelled room, is a real live Oompah Band. They're wearing lederhosen and those funny little green felt Heidi-hats with the feather in the hatband. The concertina player's lederhosen are held up with the most beautiful baumalerei-style embroidered leather braces, worn over a Jethro Tull t-shirt. Achtung baby, rock 'n roll.

I spot a group of friends sitting at a long wooden table which seems to be made of heavy railway sleepers, or oak, or whatever wood they use in Austria for their beer garden tables. Almost falling over my own ski boots—have you ever walked in ski boots? - I make my way over to the rowdy group of South African revellers. Ski boots are awful to walk in—they have absolutely no give, they're so hard, you clomp around in them looking like a waddling duck and your feet smell awful after spending a day in them.

By the time I've had my first glass of gluhwein Peter and Dane clomp in. Dane is, as all teenage boys are, quite embarrassed by his father who has no coordination whilst trying to stay upright on a set of skis. But good son that he is, he sticks with his Pa, making sure he gets to his destination. The kid knows what's good for him. He's rewarded with some Schillings.

Peter downs the first of a good few beers, waitered on by a buxom Austrian woman. She is dressed in a traditional outfit. Swirly black skirt and a tightly corseted bodice over a white blouse which is cut very low, allowing her rather large breasts to bounce up and down as she stomps through the room, six quarts of beer in each hand. We call her Griselda for the rest of the evening even though it's probably not her name. I am quite certain, however, that she is used to such irritating tourists as we are, shouting every now and then in our best German, "hey Griselda, ve vant anudda tsvai biere and sex gluhweins very much bitte".

"How're you going to get down the hill later?" Mary shouts over the music to Peter. She's in the same ski school class so she knows he's been given the boot, so to speak.

"Kevin's going to help me," Peter replies, thumbing across the table to Mary's husband. Kevin is a star skier, often spending all day on the black runs in the mountains.

"He is?" I ask, intrigued at how Kevin, who by this stage is six sheets to the wind and singing *Khum Bai Ja My Lord* at the top of his voice while the Oompah Band is still rocking out *auf, auf zum froelichen jagen*, is going to manage to get my poor unbalanced man down a ski slope... *nogal* in the dark.

Kevin suddenly gets quite serious, squints (to focus on his wife's beautiful face) and says rather indignantly, "Pete'sch tjust goin' ta stand ontha back of my schkish and Ah'll schki down to tha h'tel". Hic.

Kevin is South African. He just sounds Austrian because he's *poeg-eyed*.

Come time to make our way down the mountain, I too am feeling slightly the worse for wear. I've had more gluhwein tonight than I've had collectively in the last thirty-some years.

It's dark outside. I can hardly see my boots as I strap them into my skis and look around for Graham (another expert skier) who is going to lead us newbies down the mountain. Like I said, in the dark. *Nogal*. There are no highway lights on this alpine slope. The only lights I see are from the Landhauses and restaurants way down in the distance.

Peter and Kevin have fallen down. That's not because they're on Kevin's skis yet, but because they're both pickled. The two giggle like naughty little boys with one shouting *"ag nee man"* and the other blowing bubbles which sounds like *"jirre got gert,"* because he's fallen, face down in the snow.

Mary, Dane and I line up behind Graham. Anyway, I've washed my hands of my husband who'd been dancing with some Scandinavian blonde all night. She was 6 feet tall, muscular and ice-blue-eyed, as all Scandinavian blondes are. And she probably skied like a champ, as all Scandinavian blondes do. Feh. When she pointed at him and said, "I vant choo to dance vit me," neither of us argued. I put my ski-boot clad foot firmly in his back, shoved hard and said "she vants choo, go, go, before she vants me too!"

Following Graham down the slope (did I mention in the dark?) Peter and Kevin's histrionics get quieter the further away we get. The mountain air is crisp and almost hurts my lungs as I breathe. It's minus 4 degrees and fresh snow has started falling.

I can hear the quiet swish-swish of Graham's skis in front of me, the snow gently being pushed aside by my own skis and the crackle of ice every now and then as we hit a hard patch. It's quiet as we ski downwards, each of us concentrating on the lights in the distance.

We make it down easily to the Après Ski Bar at the bottom of the slope. The vibe there is electric. Doef-doef music is blaring. Young guys are gyrating with very cute ski bunnies in skimpy tanks, their ski suit tops peeled down to their waists, drinks in their hands and heads swaying side to side, eyes half-closed. Austrian house music is exactly the same as American, South African, British and Mongolian house music. It all has the same 4/4 beat, top-hat cymbals and synthesized bass lines with four chord changes. Doef doef... C... F... D... G... Doef doef... C... F... D... G...

Mary and Dane bugger off to bed. I stand and watch the mountain, trying to see if I can spot Peter and Kevin coming down the slopes. My head is beating in time with the music and I squint into the distance, but I don't spot them. I look up and see the most beautiful array of stars in the dark clear sky. Up to the right I notice the slope tractors clearing the snow for the next day's skiers, their headlights just barely visible behind the tree breaks.

Graham, our fearless let's-get-you-down-the-nursery-slopes leader, heads into the Après Ski Bar, squeezing past, and eyeing all those tight-assed, big-breasted, ditsy ski bunnies. Typical newly divorced man, he's only after one thing.

A Vodka Feige.

This liqueur can be enjoyed on its own, or with a mix. I'm told it brings out the cocktail maker in you. As its name reveals, it is a shot of vodka with fig. Or a fig with a shot of vodka. Either way, that vodka soaked fig is just delicious. And very, very dangerous.

I like Vodka Feige. Particularly when mixed with Red Bull. And even better, I like two vodka Feige's with Red Bull. Not together. One after the other. Especially on a cold night when I'm standing in the snow, in the dark (yes really!) waiting for my drunken-bum of a husband while listening to doef-doef achtung baby music.

About four vodka Feiges later, maybe it was five, or six, I spot Kevin skiing down the slope, coming straight down like a bat out of hell, not carving neatly as he is known to do. He's on his own. No Peter. As he gets nearer, I see he has Peter's skis slung over his shoulders. I anticipate him swishing to a halt in front of me, alas; Kevin zooms right past, straight over the road, between two landhauses, up the culvert and back down through the rest of the village, ignoring my shouts of "Oy, where'sch mah husch-band?"

Graham comes up behind me, whistling to Kevin who's long gone, leaving a trail of spray in his wake. Silently he hands me another drink. By this stage, my poor heart with its wonky mitral valve is taking some strain with all the Red Bull I'm slugging. So I drink the vodka, eat the fig and give the tin of Red Bull right back to him.

Oh, you want to know what happened to Peter, do you?

Well, the next morning, sitting at the breakfast table, sipping very hot coffee, looking quite suspiciously at the greasy bacon and eggs in front of him, and feeling very hung-over, he said, "So there we were, Kevin 'n me. Every time I got on the back of his skis and we'd just get going, he'd wobble and we'd fall over. We tried a dozen times. Kevin finally said it was a bad idea so I started walking down the slope. Problem is, I kept falling as I walked. Lucky Justyn arrived (he was coming *up* the mountain to find us) and he walked with me back down to the Landhaus."

"But darling," I breathed gently for I too was rather hung-over, sipping very hot coffee, looking quite suspiciously at the greasy bacon and eggs on *my* plate and feeling like the end of the world was nigh, "why did Kevin keep falling over then? I thought he was such a good skier?"

"He is," Peter said through a tentative mouthful of toast, "he just forgot to tighten his boots to his skis so he wasn't hooked in. That's why he kept falling over."

We didn't see Kevin and Mary again at the Hinterhag Alm that holiday in Austria. Mind you, we didn't go back up the T-bar to the Hinterhag Alm ourselves either.

That's because Dane too went MIA when we suggested another evening of revelry up there.

We so enjoyed our time in Saalbach that first skiing holiday that we ended up there again a few years later. This time, we had the full house—with all four our boys. Dane and Justyn had learnt to ski the Austrian way. Gregory and Wade had learnt to ski while we on holiday in the Pocono's, Pennsylvania the previous Christmas. They'd had a quick one-hour lesson and before you could say 'pizza' the two were whizzing down the slopes with Wade even 'ramping' off the edges of the runs. Gregory's ski poles got in the way causing him to fall often, so I took them from him and before long the two of us were zooming down Lover's Lane and trying our luck at some of the more difficult runs. They were, however, nothing compared to the runs in the Saalbach-Hinterglemm valley.

Peter and I decided to give up on the skiing thing one afternoon, opting to 'clean our room'. This was code for we're going to read a book slash have a sleep slash have nooky.

Strict instructions were given to the boys. They had to stick together in pairs. They were, after all, just wee ones. Dane was the eldest at sixteen with Gregory bringing up the rear at just seven, going on thirty.

Justyn and Gregory went off and spent the afternoon on the nursery slopes where they both felt comfortable, up the T-bar, whizz down, up the T-bar, whizz down, stop for a hot chocolate, up the T-bar, whizz down.

Dane and Wade were far more adventurous, deciding to take on some of the more difficult runs, ending in a cross-country ski back to our Landhaus.

As only generally happens in cartoons, Wade was skiing; looking back at Dane who was shouting "watch out there's a pole" and, as also generally only happens in cartoons, he skied, wide-legged, right into the pole. We sat at the dinner table laughing at their recount of how Wade had pulled this trick. The tears were rolling down our cheeks as Dane was relating the story. Then then I thought I was really going to wet myself when Dane said, "And Mommy, Wade got up and I asked him if he was ok. He was winded, but he said, Dane, I hurt my thorax but lucky I didn't hurt my testicles."

The next day, Peter invested in a sled. Remember, Peter had been expelled from ski-school years before, but he really wanted to join in the fun. So, as the rest of the gang were skiing down the slopes, Peter was keeping up with us, just without skis attached to his feet. His sled reminded me of my Triang tricycle when I was around four or five. Peter's sled had skis on both sides and came complete with an independent front ski attached to a steering wheel and easy-to-use brakes. Problem was, I think the sled was actually made for kids. Peter's knees were up round his neck when he sat on the thing which resulted in him not being able to use those brakes. So instead, he would put his feet out and dig his heels in. And that's how he stopped. Quite suddenly most of the time. Justyn, who was right behind him, went sraight up his gezunta pipe and broke the tip of Peter's coccyx with the tip of his Salomons.

That night, at the dinner table, Peter, who was sitting askew on a feather pillow from our bed, asked, "Who wants to give up skiing for a few days?"

I could see a couple of hands wanting to go up. The kids weren't sure of where this would lead though so they tentatively kept their hands under the table. I put mine up high and said, "I'm *gatvol* of everyone getting hurt. I need a break."

Four sets of hands shot up.

Within the hour we found ourselves on the road to visit Granny and Opa in Holland.

THE WHITE ASHES OF KUIKDUIN

We never realised that the surprise visit we paid to the family in Holland that year would be the last New Year we would see in with Peter's father.

He was a simple man. At his happiest when he was eating a good piece of Dutch boerenkaas or drinking a Heineken beer. Also happy when he switched off his hearing aid and didn't have to listen to his wife nagging him to go check the post, feed the dog, switch off the lights and so forth.

My father-in-law liked me. He would walk past me and give me a pinch on the bum and then pretend it wasn't him, shoving his nose up into the air and whistling a little ditty. He loved coming to visit us as Peter would give him as much beer as he could possibly consume, and I baked fresh bread daily for his breakfast. He did not like shop-bought bread which he said was 'airy-fairy'.

My mother-in-law didn't really like me. That's ok. She was entitled to her opinions, but she sure missed out on a lot by being so full of shit.

So, the day we all left Saalbach, some with sore thoraxes others with broken coccyx's, I settled down in the front seat of the Vito and watched the snow falling around us. It was mesmerising. I love winter, I love the cold and I especially love the snow.

The boys snoozed in the back of the car, lulled to sleep by the warmth of the Mercedes heater and full tummies from the dinner we had neatly abandoned.

Fourteen hours later, we pulled into the driveway of Peter's cousins' house in Den Haag, Holland. We had stopped at the local bakery and purchased traditional *olie bollen* and *apel flap* for our New Year celebrations.

I am so grateful that we took that drive. The surprise on Peter's Dad's face will be a treasured memory for years. I think he knew his end was near and to have his son and his grand-children around him was, I am positive, a blessing. He took me to one side and whispered in his faint Dutch accent, "When I die, please bring me back to Holland." I promised him solemnly that we would do so, not knowing that just two months later, he would pass away.

The morning we were leaving South Africa to return to Cairo after the funeral service, I drove silently and quietly out of the Crematorium gates, a small wooden casket with my father-in-law's ashes resting gently on the seat next to me. Neither Peter nor his sister could face going to fetch the ashes, so, being the only one in the family who was capable of doing so, I found myself talking to the box.

"Ok, Father, so we're going to Egypt tonight, then in about a month's time, we'll take you to Holland. Where do you want us to scatter you? Amsterdam? No? Ok. Um, Schijveningen? No? Ok. Ahhh, oooh, Kuikduin! Good place, Dad."

It's highly illegal (and one can end up with a criminal record) for carrying the ashes of a person over the borders without the proper documentation. Which I didn't have. I popped the casket into the bottom of my vanity bag and carried my father-in-law onto Egypt Air with me. The Egyptian check-in staff looked the other way. Fortunately they were happy to have their palms crossed with a couple of cases of their favourite beverage from Meesda Beeda from Cairo.

I did exactly the same thing when we left Cairo for Amsterdam a couple of months later. Popped Dad into my vanity bag. And not once was I asked by any border patrol person exactly what the sandy looking stuff in the bottom of my case was. If they had asked, I doubt they would have believed me if I said it was Fuller's Earth which you mixed up for a facial masque, hey?

I could see Peter was nervous the morning we were going to do the deed. He'd been procrastinating about getting out of bed, using every excuse he could think of. From "it looks like it's going to rain" to "can I please have another cup of coffee". So I took the bull by the horns and cajoled him into driving me up to the local shopping centre where we could have breakfast and I could go into the florist. There, I bought three beautiful long stemmed red roses. One for John's wife, one for his daughter and one for the son who would scatter his ashes back into his home soil.

We pulled up at a remote spot away from the shops of Kuikduin and the prying eyes of strangers. The wind was whispering gently along the shoreline, the waves lapping at the edge of the beach. The sky was a royal blue, not a cloud to be seen. So much for rain.

We trekked across the dunes to a secluded spot, carrying the casket with gentle reverence. Peter knelt down and lifted the lid. Inside was a plastic packet with the earthly remains of his father. He looked up at me. I could see the question 'what do I do next' etched across his forehead. Gently, and in silence, I took his hand. Together we reached into the packet, picked up a handful of the ashes and scattered them on the dunes.

Then we placed the three red roses there as a token of our love for the man who we had brought home.

He Coloured My Life

I am the sum of the people who have influenced my life in some way or the other. Mostly, I believe my formative years were not set in stone (as experts suggest) before the age of six, but rather the couple of years that I lived, as a teenager, with my sister and her husband.

If ever there was a man who fathered me, as a father would, it was Peter van Hees.

There is no disrespect meant to my real father here, but when my mother died, he palmed me off on my sister. Only because, I think, he didn't know what to do with a fourteen year old girl. As I grew older, I realised that my father was probably gay and had only married my mother to save face—as homosexuals did in those days. He loved me, I am sure of that, but he didn't know how to be a father to a young teenage girl.

Which Peter van Hees did. That is his real name. I have not concealed his identity in my memoir because I use it with the highest respect and admiration to pay homage to the man who would become more to me than I could ever imagine.

At thirty-five, Peter took a scrawny fourteen year old and showed me more encouragement and acceptance than any of the other family members had in the years before.

It was he who taught me to clay-pigeon shoot. It was he who bought me, and then taught me, to ride a motor bike. He taught me funny poems which I still remember and which I recited to my children when they were babes. He taught me the value of family life, of living, of loving, of compassion and care, of fun and laughter, of being there without question.

He taught me to have the courage of my convictions. And I thank him from the bottom of my heart which occasionally skips a beat. Because I love him.

⁓

At fourteen years old himself, Pete was returning home from boarding school with his elder brother. They were on a train bound for the mining town of Welkom where his father worked as a shift boss on the gold mines. Peter's mother was a nursing sister at the newly built municipal hospital.

The train pulled into the station.

"I can't walk!" Peter said to his brother as he tried to get up from the seat in the compartment they had just spent the last eighteen hours in.

"What do you mean, you can't walk?"

"I can't feel my legs!" he cried.

His brother carried him to the waiting car. They rushed him home for the local doctor to see during his house rounds. No actual diagnosis was made at that time other than the young boy's legs were put into callipers to stop them trembling, and he was confined to a wheelchair after a lengthy hospital stay. He was diagnosed a paraplegic. Nowadays, with advanced medicine and science, we know that he had actually suffered a neurological attack of transverse myelitis and had contracted Devics Disease.

Despite his disability, Peter did everything a young man could do—except walk. This did not deter him from finishing his school years and opening an engineering company with his older brother. He was a very handsome young man who dated quite a few girls. Instead of relying on others to fetch and carry, he adjusted his cars foot controls so that he could drive himself to fetch his dates.

Peter met my sister, Alma, shortly after my parents arrived in Welkom from Namibia. My father had accepted a contract at the up-and-coming airport just outside of Welkom. It was the boom years with many gold mines springing up in the area. They produced vast amounts of gold and twice a day a Dakota would fly down from Johannesburg, deposit its passengers, mostly mining bosses, and return with a full load of gold bars in its hold.

Along with a cat, a wife and an eight year old daughter, my father introduced Alma and her three month old baby into Welkom society.

Alma's first husband had disappeared, leaving her pregnant. They had had a brief fling as young teenagers, resulting in an unplanned pregnancy and a forced marriage. Which is what parents did in those days. Force young people to marry. Mainly to save face. The young man wasn't happy at finding himself tied to a pregnant girl he hardly knew and so, after a couple of months, he left. Left Alma holding the baby, so to speak. Which Peter van Hees would adopt and bring up as his own. Their wedding was the talk of the town. The beautiful young divorcee and the paraplegic. People whispered that she was just in it for the money. He was handsome, he was wealthy, but, they said, he couldn't walk, what was in it for her? Give Alma her due. She loved him. He adored the baby, he adored his wife. They bought a house and they were happy.

Or so we all thought.

Now one should never speak ill of the dead, but believe you me, I don't want to lie about them either. My sister, I suspect, was loony. She had everything. A husband who treated her royally, a beautiful big house, fancy cars, aeroplanes (which she piloted herself), and a life many would have given their left tits for.

She blew it all against the wall by screwing around with other men and eventually they divorced.

The first thing Peter realised when I went to live with them was that I had no independence. I had been dependant on my parents for so long, now I was dependent on him and my sister. He took me to a motorbike shop one afternoon after school.

"Sit on that one," he instructed me. I sat.

"Do you like it?" he asked. I liked. I've always loved red and the metallic paintwork of the bike shone and blinked and I liked.

"Put it on the back of the *bakkie* and take it home," he said to Alfred, the driver from his engineering company.

The man who bought me a motorbike so that I could become independent also gave me the gift of freedom, freedom to ride the road and to enjoy the many miles I would ride in my life.

The second thing he did was to give me pocket money. I got R10.00 a week. From that I had to make sure that my bike was filled with petrol and oil. The rest I could do with as I pleased.

"Close the accelerator, pull the clutch in and put it into gear with your foot!" Peter shouted down the road as I tried my best to get the little red Kawasaki to stop revving so high. He was wheeling himself next to me as he taught me to ride.

"Which one's the clutch?" I shouted back at him, but with the noise of the small engine whining in my ears, all I could see was his mouth moving and his arms pushing frenetically at the steel rims of his wheels.

Around and around the oval we went, Peter pushing and shouting, me revving and braking, skidding and nearly seeing my you-know-what. Before long, I was zooming off to the shops to buy bread and milk for my sister.

"Trischa," she'd shout from the kitchen, "please go to the café and buy me some smokes."

I was willing to go shopping many times for her. It meant I could ride my bike. Until I had my learners licence, though, I was not allowed on the main roads. We lived in a community outside of Welkom which had more dirt roads than tar. I was allowed to ride on those. So, when Alma needed me to go to the shops, I hoppity skittled and scooted off, happy as a pig in shit.

I got my learners licence on my sixteenth birthday. That was the start of many miles of riding my bike around Welkom, going backwards and forwards to school during the week and then to town on a Saturday morning where I would meet my friend Abigail. She would sit in the very back booth of the Horseshoe Inn with her pot of tea and a pack of twenty cigarettes which she would smoke. She held court there the whole morning, with various people coming and going, sliding into the booth for a fag and a chat.

I had a sickening crush on Abi's brother, Alan. He was only a year ahead of me at school, but I thought he was just magnificent. He was olive-skinned with dark hair, wisps of which curled at his ears. His eyes were smoky. He was tall and lean.

Unfortunately, he liked older women and so he was most definitely not interested in me. That didn't stop me from following him around like a love-sick puppy though. I was desperate for him to ask me to a dance, or a disco, or a movie. He never did and I was devastated each time I'd hear that he was taking some other girl to the Saturday evening socials. He did, however, ask me to go with him to the salt pan at the back of our village. To scramble. That's because when we got there, he would hop off his 50cc Honda and swap me for my 90cc which he would then ride the hell out of, throwing up sand and salt while I tried hard to keep up on his piece of shit.

Then we'd get back to the house, lie on the front lawn while he smoked a fag before going home.

He was not the first crush to use and abuse me.

LEMON IS NOT THE NAME
OF MY FIRST CRUSH

My first real crush was on Peter van Hees' cousin, Steven. He was about three years older than me and, at age seventeen, had no interest in a skinny flat-chested girl with knobbly knees and big ginger freckles.

We had arrived at Peter's holiday home in Port Alfred where we would spend most of the summer holidays, fishing on the Cowie River, catching crabs and holding Wicks bubble gum competitions. Peter never used to shave while on holiday. As he said, he was on holiday too, so why shave? So, when he had chewed his bubble gum for long enough that it was soft and warm and pliable, he would blow the most ginormous bubbles I'd ever seen in my life. They'd be so big they'd obscure his entire face. Of course the inevitable would happen. Someone would sneak up behind his chair and, with forefinger and thumb, would pinch that bubble and it would pop. Fine strands of pink gum bits would have to be picked out of his prickly beard, eyebrows and even his hairline. It didn't stop us from chewing gum and blowing bubbles

44

most nights, sitting outside the back door on the *stoep* enjoying the summer heat.

We had a little boat with an outboard motor in which we'd go fishing. First, Peter would scoot out of his chair onto the side of the jetty, Steven would lodge the chair into the boat and then pick Peter up and place him back into his chair, now securely wedged so that he wouldn't topple out of the boat. The three of us drank copious amounts of Old Brown Sherry on those fishing trips. At night we'd go out and catch crabs, during the days it was spotted grunters and baby sharks.

We also had an old Landrover which was housed in the hangar at the airport. We'd fly in with my sister piloting her 6-seater Beechcraft Bonanza, park the plane in the hangar and toss our gear into the Landy. No need for Avis Rentals in those days.

Steven was washing the Landrover. Of course I was trying to get his attention. I had a crush on him, didn't I?

"I'll throw mud on the Landy," I teased, prancing around, swinging my hips side-to-side.

"Don't even think about it, Patricia." He warned me.

"And what will you do if I do throw mud on it?" again I tried the teasing thing, smiling and fluttering my eyelashes. *Fooitog*, I shudder now to think of it.

"I'll rub your face right in that pool of mud," he answered, pointing at a puddle which had formed from a leak in the hosepipe.

I didn't believe him, or if I did, I figured at least a face rubbing in the mud was better than being ignored. So I slapped a huge handful of watery sand right onto the bonnet of the Landy - which had of course just been washed and dried.

And I got a face-rubbing of note. The mud went up my nostrils, down the back of my throat; it was smudged in my ears and down my top. My niece was so upset by this that she jumped on Steven's back and started beating him with her little six year old fists shouting, "You bladdy, bladdy, bladdy!"

As I stood in the bathroom, washing the mud from my eyes and nose, I realised then that any thoughts I might have had of a summer holiday romance was just pie in the sky.

"I'll get you back!" I hiccoughed through my tears.

As I mentioned before, I'm feisty. I'm also conniving, and I can wait and pounce when the timing is right.

One late afternoon that same holiday, Steven and I walked down to the river together with strict instructions from Alma to go catch crabs. Of the variety that you can eat. She was *lis* for fresh crab for dinner. The weather had turned a little and it was quite chilly. The clouds were thick and heavy, promising a typical late summer afternoons' drenching.

Steven hoisted the outboard motor onto the dinghy. I got into the boat and settled down.

"Don't let the boat drift too much that I can't hop in, Trisch," he said, untying the ropes, "hold on to the side of the jetty."

My promise to 'get him back' flashed across my eyes. This was an opportunity I couldn't miss. I could feel the red horns pushing out from under my forehead and a tail to match tickling my rear end. I wiggled with anticipation. Just as he grabbed hold of the boat, I let go of the jetty. The tide in the river was fast. The water took hold of the dinghy and pulled it away from the edge of the riverbank. It was a moment of great enjoyment for me. There was Steven, splayed out over the water, hands clutching the side of the dinghy, with his toes gripping the edge of the jetty. A cartoon moment of note.

Guess what happened?

I got him back.

HARLEY THE TIME TO GO PINK NOW IS IT?

For some unknown reason my friend, Julie Purkis asked me to do a motivational talk at a Breast Cancer Ride.

"But Julie, I haven't had breast cancer," I answered, "how could I possibly address people on the subject?"

"Trisch, we all know you have the gift of the gab, you're a cancer survivor too, so you're just the perfect person to do this."

"OK, but... ride? I don't do horses!" I cast my eyes heavenward. What on earth would make her think I was part of the mink and manure brigade?

"And anyway," I carried on breathlessly thinking of those smelly things they measure in hands - why? Isn't metric good enough? - trampling all over my new *takkies* and blowing hot hay-scented air over my Cartier fragranced body, "I'm just not sure how to make a woman feel good when she's facing such an awful thing like losing a breast."

And so our conversation went, me backing off, Julie lunging forward, parrying to and fro until one of us just had to win. I lost.

The horses I had in mind were nowhere near the horse power Julie was talking about. Harley and horse in the same thought process just didn't connect in my brain. Eventually I experienced the Aha! Moment. That one light bulb could have lit up a thousand Christmas trees without any electricity when the penny fell into this blonde's slot.

The Ladies of Harley in Pretoria were raising funds for a Breast Cancer Awareness group by riding out on a Sunday morning to a restaurant in Broederstroom for breakfast. Julie wanted us to join in the pack ride. One small, oh all right, 1450-horse-power problem. I didn't ride a Harley. Which clearly wasn't a problem for her. Smart girl, she had all the aces up her tattoo-painted body-stockinged wicked-Harley-chick sleeve.

I trundled off home to my darling husband and told him what we were going to be doing that coming Sunday.

"Sweetheart," I schmoozed. He looked up from his Sudoku puzzle very briefly and I could see his brain scheming 'hmmmm I wonder how much this is going to cost me'? Little did he know, poor soul.

"You remember my friend Julie?" I continued, swaying side to side—just like a cobra before it strikes you understand, "the one who rides a Harley? The one whose sister-in-law is battling breast cancer?"

"Hrrumph," came back the reply while one hand flicked away the remnants of the eraser bits from the Sudoku book, the other twiddling the HB clutch-pencil. I could see that I'd interrupted his train of thought and that 9 should have not been 9. Oh nein! 9 should have been 6.

"Well," I continued, "Julie's riding with her friends this Sunday and she wants me to talk about breast cancer and then we'll have breakfast with them and then they'll bring us back home and it'll be this Sunday and we have to get up early, and you have to wear a pink shirt...and...and... and..." I rattled on.

Peter's eyes flew open, the pupils doing a spiral thing like you see in the cartoons when the character's lost the plot or been *bliksemed* and is seeing little blue birdies going tjeep-tjeep in a circle above its head.

"You got breast cancer?" he spluttered, "you going to lose your titties?"

"Oh my Gawd, no!" I slapped at him. And there I thought he was panicked about wearing pink.

He sighed a huge sigh of relief, flopped back on the couch and pencilled in 5 in 5's space. Clever man.

Over dinner that evening, which was a particularly good steak as only we can get steak in South Africa, with a delicious black crushed pepper-corn sauce, lightly blanched asparagus and salad, we talked through the coming Sunday's plans.

Peter had ridden motorbikes in his youth and we were both quite excited to be taking part in a Harley ride. Peter had ridden 'superbikes' while I'd had enjoyed a fairly long stint on my little red Kawasaki. A nasty fall off a bigger off-road scrambler some years later had put paid to my bike riding in my early adulthood. Also I think being pregnant probably had something to do with it too.

"So how're we going to get there?" Peter asked through a mouthful of tender rump.

"Umm," I swallowed, "we'll go to the Mugg & Bean in our car, then they'll put us on the back of two bikes and we'll ride pillion to the event."

"Not a shit!" he exclaimed, slamming his fork onto his plate causing the rump to go one way and the salad to go the other. The kitties pounced on the rump, possibly thinking, 'weee! It's raining rump, hallelujah!'

"There's no way I'm getting on the back of a bike if I'm not riding it myself!"

And so it came to be that on the Saturday afternoon before the ride took place, a huge, beautiful, shiny black and chrome Harley-Davidson was parked in our garage, ready to ride.

"Alastair!" Peter shouted down the phone line. You'd think Alastair was in Outer Mongolia, when in actual fact, if Peter had stepped out of our garage, taken 40 steps down the road and turned left at the gate sporting the "Dogs… Keep The F*ck Out" sign, he could have knocked on Al's front door.

But there he was, on the phone to Al. "I need a bike for Sunday, pal."

Al. Pal. If he'd been such a good pal, he'd never have let us onto a bike, never mind a mind-blowing, powerful Harley-Davidson.

Al was the Johannesburg Chapter Director of HOG (Harley Owners Group) and Chairman of a touring company which hired out Harleys. Which is exactly what he did for us. Hire us a Harley. And which is why this beautiful very shiny black and chrome *thing* was parked in our garage on that Saturday night, complete with helmets, gloves and jackets.

Early Sunday morning, even before the birds had half a chance to chirp, Peter and I flew out of our garage, skidded around the corner and took off up the driveway. Harley's are powerful bikes and Peter hadn't ridden since he was about twenty two. Actually, he had never ridden a Harley and riding one requires a very different skill set to riding a 'normal' bike. We careered around the corner at Number 4, passed Le-le-le-Lucas the security guard, who had such a shocked look on his face at seeing Mister Peter on a bike, and vamoosed onto the main road. You see, Lucas was used to seeing Mister Peter; hair slicked back, sunglasses covering his light-sensitive eyes and Pavarotti blaring from the CD player, in his little silver SLK with the roof down.

This was putting wind in Peter's hair in an entirely different fashion.

We made it to Pretoria in one piece. We made it to Broederstroom in another piece. Then we put the pieces together and decided this Harley thing was actually quite *lekker*.

By the time we got home later that day, Peter was already negotiating the purchase of the bike with Al. You know, Al? Our pal? Al's touring company wanted to sell some of their bikes, so the Electra Glide which had ousted my poor little Toyota from my side of the double garage, was winking at Peter and whispering "buy me, buy me!' And Peter, wimp that he was, was not arguing with that beautiful big black shiny thing that went brr-bop-bop as its two pistons connected to the twin v-arranged cylinders, firing at uneven intervals.

The two men settled on a deal, shook hands and opened beers to celebrate. This is a typical South African boy thing. The minute a deal is struck, they open the beers. Now I hate the taste of beer and would have been so much happier had they opened a good bottle of the finest red our country's vineyards had to offer. But there they were, clinking green glass bottle necks while standing in the garage admiring Peter's new acquisition which was also still going pink-pink-pink as the engine cooled down.

"Hang on just one moment, Mister!" I declared, one hand on hip, the other arm outstretched with palm facing outwards and the forefinger pointing skywards, doing that cobra head-swaying thing.

Both boys stopped in mid-slug, slowly lowered their beers, and, in unison, said "whaaaaat?"

"If you're buying that *thing* and you're going to be riding it, and you think I'm going to be riding on the back with you," I paused for dramatic effect, "you are sorely mistaken."

"Awww, Trischa," said the one who'd just paid a whole bunch of money for said *thing*, while the other was already expounding the excitement of riding pillion with statements like "just ask..."

"You are sorely mistaken!" I interrupted again, "I said I will not be riding with you, Peter. I will be riding my own."

The colour of Al's irises, one blue, one brown, a-la-David-Bowie, turned dollar sign green as I asked him if he had a Harley to sell to me.

Within an hour, another beautiful big black and chrome shiny Harley parked its cheeky rear end next to the other one in the garage and my poor little Toyota blinked its flickers and resigned itself to having been ousted from its secure parking spot.

So that, as they say in the history books, is how I became a pink Harley chick. *And it's all your fault, Julie Purkis!*

PURPLE PEOPLE EATERS

I have four boys. Two I birthed; two I *erfed*. They're all grown up now and I'm still not a Granny. A whaaaat? Here's a fifty-one year old Harley chick *kvetching* about not being a Granny? I should have my head read.

Dane, being the eldest, always got the short end of the stick. He did stuff first, so he got into terrible trouble all the time. By the time Gregory did the same thing, we were like *'been there, done that'* so Greg didn't get into half the shit poor old Dane did. The two in the middle, Justyn and Wade, sailed through their childhoods, ducking under Peter's radar. Clever boys.

We travelled the world with those four boys and I became quite adept at organising them. Each would get a packing list. Two pairs of jeans. Two jerseys. One jacket. Four t-shirts. Six pairs of underpants (please make sure they don't have holes in them). Six pairs of socks (ditto). One toothbrush, toothpaste, soap, deodorant, hairbrush. Put these in your toiletry bag. No toys, no guns (plastic or otherwise) and leave the Blu-Tack at home. We don't want security officials thinking you've got plastic explosives in your moonbags.

The boys would pack their suitcases and tick off the list under the heading *packed at home*. Then, each time we'd leave a stopover, they'd have to make sure they had everything packed in their bags and tick off the list under the heading *checked that I got it*.

You think this helped? Not a bit. We still ended up with socks without a mate or a missing jersey which had been left on a bus/train/plane. What worried me most was when a boy arrived home with clothing in his bag that I had never seen before and which had not been acquired through a credit card purchase at a reputable store along our travels.

Having two sets of boys, one set his, one set mine, was quite complicated initially. As all divorced parents understand, the my-weekend your-weekend routine can sometimes be stuffed up by malicious exes who don't want their kids to spend time with your new partners' kids. This is terribly self-centered and I despised my ex-husband for always trying to cock up our weekends, especially as the boys mostly enjoyed each other's company.

From, I suppose, another viewpoint (some would say self-centered too), it gave Peter and I the opportunity to explore our own relationship when we had alternate weekends without the children.

But the times we had all the kids together, we tried to make as much fun as possible.

One weekend, Justyn and Gregory arrived at our house sans slippers and gowns. Under normal circumstances this wouldn't have been a problem because I'm not the type of mother to worry about boys running around barefoot in their PJ's. But Justyn's birth mother was quite pedantic and would send six pairs of everything for a two night stay. Needless to say, they usually went home with these items unworn and Peter would be in serious shit the following week because, according to her, he wasn't looking after his sons properly. Meow. Did I just say all that?

This particular weekend, however, the no-slipper thing posed a huge problem. Justyn's front milk tooth had fallen out at dinner time. It had been loose for a while and with just enough tongue action, he managed to get the last little thread of gum holding it in his mouth to snap. Then he panicked because it bled and then he panicked even more when he realised he had no slipper to put the tooth in for the tooth mouse to collect.

In our house the tooth mouse was a very generous fellow and each of the kids eagerly looked forward to counting the dosh they would find in their slippers. Some would use it to buy CDs, some would save it, but Justyn would take it to school the next week and blow it on candy, cold drinks, candy and more candy. He had such a sweet tooth it's a wonder he didn't lose more quicker.

So having no slippers with him was a very scary thought for this panicked little six year old. I tried to tell him it was ok, just leave the tooth next to the bed on the nightstand and I was sure the mouse would find it. But he wasn't having any of that. In his little mind, the tooth mouse would only find it if it was nestled in a slipper placed on the carpet at the side of his bed.

Wade to the rescue. Being very pragmatic, Wade understood exactly Justyn's anxiety, having just recently lost a tooth himself. He thus proffered his own slipper to his older step-brother.

"Justyn," he said very solemnly, with one slipper outstretched in his little hand, "you can use my slipper to put your tooth in tonight. I'm sure the tooth mouse will think it's your slipper."

"I promise I'll give it back to you in the morning," a very relieved little boy answered, "and I'll buy you a sucker with the money the tooth mouse leaves me."

"Ag, that's ok, Justyn. You don't have to buy me a sucker. But just make sure the tooth mouse doesn't poop in my slipper, ok?"

Ok!

⁓

Our four boys were, I thank G-d every day, all very different.

Wade was a plodder. He was never going to be a rocket scientist. He told me so one day. When I asked him what he wanted to be when he grew up, he said, "A motor mac." And today, at 25, he is not only a qualified motor mechanic, but an amazingly talented re-builder of race cars. Oh, and Volkswagen Beetles. He is making a name for himself in the industry as a reliable and hard-working young man and I am so incredibly proud of him.

Wade can sniff out a party. From the time he started going out in his own car, he would come home in the early hours of the morning and, when asked what he'd got up to, he'd respond with 'I went to a party, Ma' even though that wasn't where he was headed the previous evening.

He is just over six foot and has a beautiful open face which clearly stands him in good stead with the young ladies. He is not shy and has a host of opening-lines which obviously aren't corny. If they are, then the chicks he pulls with them are dim. I don't think Wade minds though. He's not looking for a life-time mate; he's just enjoying the mating thing while he's still young and virile.

His head is squarely on his shoulders and he is a walking encyclopaedia when it comes to anything to do with motor car engines. Nowadays, when a car in our family needs attention, we take it to Wade. When we need to buy a new car, we ask Wade to look it over before we make our final decision. And, for a bottle of Captain Morgan Gold, Wade will change the sparkplugs on Dane's little scooter, Miss Muriel.

Justyn was a complex little guy who turned to his PC and food for comfort. We always knew he would do something with computers and today has his own small business, implementing networks and repairing computers. He's not so little anymore. Justyn ate his way through troubled teenage years, piling on not only his Freshman Fifteen, but another fifty on top of that too. He spent his last three years of High School in Austria where schnitzel and fries was his staple diet. MacDonald's and Lindt were also on the hit list.

At twenty seven, Justyn finally realized his weight issue was standing in his way of finding a girlfriend and so he started a controlled weight loss diet and exercise routine. I reckon once he's down to his goal weight, he will be a very handsome man. Just like his father.

Dane was always going to be a musician. Even from an early age when he would sing himself to sleep, we knew that music was the route he would take in his life. And he has, studying film scoring and composition at a highly regarded college in the USA.

He is now a well-known entertainer for a large hotel-group in South Africa. He lives on a most beautiful resort, working a couple of shifts a day. He scoots up and down to his gigs on the resort on his trusty steed, Miss Muriel. She is a dinky little blue two-stroke scooter. He parks her inside his bed-sitter when he goes out. Heaven forbid someone tried to nick her.

Gregory, my favourite little shit, was always the cutest little guy and he used that cuteness to great advantage. On average, his height, or lack thereof, brought his age down at least three years, so when he was six, people would think he was a three year old, when he was sixteen, they thought he was thirteen.

When we went to Disney in Orlando one year, Gregory knew that his height would restrict him from getting on many of the rides, so, clever kid, that he was, he purchased an Evil Queen crown from the Emporium in Main Street which gave him the extra inches needed to pass muster.

He is now, at twenty-two, a couple of inches taller than two bricks and a tickey high, but still a short-ass with short-man-syndrome. He hasn't quite got it together yet. As I write this memoir, he is still finding his feet, which are there somewhere... he just needs to look down.

SOMEWHERE OVER (THERE IS) A RAINBOW

How am I supposed to be colour-blind when I live in a rainbow nation for goodness sake?

Through the apartheid years, as I mentioned earlier on, white kids like myself were brought up pretty much believing that we were superior to the black kids who belonged to our nannies and housemaids. These kids would be allowed to play with us in the backyard of our homes, but G-d forbid they dared put a foot into the house, let alone into our playrooms and bedrooms.

How sad that as a kid I thought that these kids were dirty and stupid. Stupid me. Stupid grown-ups for teaching me to think that way.

I am privileged to have had some awesome people come into my life, great friends who are amazing entrepreneurs, brilliant scientists, creative performers. People who love me without doubt and people who I know would take a bullet for me. And they're people of colour.

But I'm not colour-blind. I just can't be. I need the vibrancy of the different hues of various skin tones to energize me. I love the fact that our country is made up of different people, different cultures, and different races. I don't like that some people want us to all be the same, though. We are not. We are a rainbow nation. In 1982 Alice Walker coined the word colorism. I like that word although I'm not mad about her description of it, despite accepting from whence it comes. She said that with racism, it is the social meaning attached to an individual's race that determines social status. With colorism it is the social meaning attached to an individual's skin colour that determines social status. Which is why, she continued, dark people turned to skin lightening techniques and inter-marriage with light skinned people.

I don't know. I like the fact that we're all different. Hell, if we were all the same, we'd live such a humdrum existence.

Despite that, I still have a hard time trying to describe a black person. Brown skin, brown eyes, black hair. Sometimes their hair is braided, sometimes it's not. Most times, the women wear wigs. And when I see blonde haired black people, I do a double take and think WTF? Now how do I describe *that*?

When I say "the black girl with the gold front tooth wearing the pink sweater," I am labelled racist. Is this because I referred to her skin colour or the colour of her sweater? Yet, when describing a white person as "the white girl with the red platform shoes and the green streaked Mohawk," that's ok, that's not racist.

I get seriously miffed when I see signboards announcing a meeting of the Black Businessman's Forum. That's ok. But don't you dare put up a sign for the White People's Cake Baking Society. That's racist. And that's not because of my skin colour. That's because I am a South African with a heap of history being shoved down my throat for an era of which I was not a part.

If referring to colour as a means of description is racist, then racism is alive and well and living in South Africa.

We all run around thinking we are democratic and liberal and that we love each other. Bullshit. There is more black-on-black violence in this country that we care to divulge. The majority of black people are still underprivileged. They still live under appalling conditions. They still live below the breadline. They still walk miles every day to earn a meagre living.

The average white person still has his or her head firmly up their bum. In the economic climate we live in, repercussions from the sanctions imposed during the apartheid years still seem unlikely to lift in a hurry. Black economic empowerment which has crippled many companies and industries, forcing whites to leave our country, is firmly entrenched with little care for those who originally set the ball rolling. People in general these days take care of their own. There is so little to go around anymore, that they truly practice the adage of charity begins at home.

Working in a charitable Foundation has opened my eyes to the scourge of HIV/AIDS and poverty which faces far too many people in our country. I have held the hands of the elderly who were dying and tried to give them comfort in their last moments. They didn't give a fig that I am a white woman. I have picked up abandoned babies and tickled them and kissed their chubby cheeks. They too don't see my colour. I have seen beautiful little blonde girls left in orphanages by their drunken mothers, growing up not being able to speak their mother tongue, dancing and singing like the black women who look after them.

In 1992, South Africa's white people voted in a referendum to lift apartheid. It was a resounding Yes! White people voted to give blacks and browns and oranges and yellows and pinks and greens and every other South African the opportunity to make this country into the rainbow nation that it is.

Now can we all please stop the bullshit that we are all the same? We are not. We are each unique in our own way.

And that's not racist, nor is it Colorist. It just is.

I'd Like to Buy The World a Red Beps

We lived in Egypt for five glorious years, thanks to the big red Coca-Cola Company. When Egypt was a cool place to live, even though the average temperature in summer took the mercury higher than 36degC. We lived there when Mubarak ran the place. Say what you want, when he was Prez, the country was calm. Everyone knew their place. The *gawagga's* (foreigners) lived the colonial life; the Egyptians lived according to the seasons. When it was hot, they wore lightweight pale blue and green *galabeya's*, when it was cold, they changed into dark greys and black.

We lived there before all the clever Egyptian kids who'd been educated in the American system along with my kids, got brains and Google and realised there was a world out there which needed to be 'upgraded' if you get my drift.

Egyptians, when they're not trying to emulate Americans, have a really interesting way of talking. They can't pronounce the letter "P". So Peter became Beeda. Meesta Beeda. We ate bobcorn at the movies and we drank Bebsi. Well not us. We were extremely loyal so we only drank Coca-Cola products.

Even flying to Greece on Olympic Airways, when offered a Pepsi, I would decline (sometimes not so gracefully either, I'm ashamed to admit) and ask for orange juice. If there was none on board, then the kids drank red wine with me. My kids learnt at a very early age to tell the difference between *kak bek* and a really good Merlot.

Egypt was a revelation. Whilst being dirty and dusty and smelly and corrupt, it represented to us *gawagga's* country club, diplomatic dinners, shopping, travelling, partying. The ex-pat life those days was a life to behold.

I took up golf at Katameya Country Club. As Peter said, I learnt to play 'dammit'. Dammit is a little white ball you try to hit without taking a rather large piece of turf out of a long green lawn at the same time. It's not like polo where it's acceptable to replace the turf and trample on it while you're enjoying a glass of champers. You don't drink champers when you're dammiting. You drink beer. Local beer called Sakkara. With bits of shit from the Nile floating around in the bottom of the bottle. Fortunately, I don't drink beer.

I swear the people who drank that stuff either had cast-iron stomachs or they were stupid. It looked disgusting. I had to find an alternative. And what an alternative I found. Assub. This is a juice, pressed fresh on the streets of Cairo. It's served at room temperature which, in the heat of summer, can sometimes reach 40 degrees. Long sticks of sugar cane are fed into an industrial metal juicer which reminded me of my mother's runner bean cutter machine. Anyhow, this juicer spits out bits of cane wood on the one side and a green juice trickles out of the other side into glass beer mugs. It is pure sugar and I loved it. No wonder I put on ten pounds while living there.

Egyptian Mango juice is also just the best. Fresh pressed from the mango groves in Ismailiya, the juice was thick and lumpy and absolutely delicious. As was the guava juice, but it was a white milky nectar. Now in South Africa our guavas are pink (aren't they all) so discovering guavas with milky white flesh took some getting used to.

I remember the first day I visited Engineer Mahmoud, the fruit and veg seller on Road Nine. By the way, just about every Egyptian I ever met was an Engineer. The flower seller was one, so was the guy who came in to change the light-bulbs in the entrance hall of the villa we lived in. Whether or not they really were Engineers remains to be proven but when Engineer Salah was at the door, I greeted him as 'Engineer Salah' even though he was only there to collect the rent.

"Berry nice goo-ava's, Madame," Engineer Mahmoud leered at me, his face close up to mine, his yellow teeth showing behind curling wet lips. His breath smelt worse than the camels we had ridden up at the pyramids of Giza the previous week.

I took a step backwards, he came forwards a step, hand outstretched with a guava in his filthy palm. In the other hand he wielded a knife, blade so sharp it could slit a throat with one easy flick. He cut off a piece of the guava and offered it to me. My stomach turned at the sight of the piece of white fruit, pearlescent and succulent, nestling in that dirty palm with fingernails so black I wondered if they even knew about, never mind used, scrubbing brushes in Egypt.

"*La, la, la, shookrun!* I have eaten today!" I cried, (no, no, no, thank you) trying to be ever-so diplomatic.

"Is good, Madame, is berry sweet," he kept coming at me.

Bless his heart, my eldest son, Dane, took one for his mom. He scooped the proffered fruit into his mouth took two chews and swallowed. His face went from ashen-white to puce-pink (which in my opinion is what the guava should have looked like anyway).

He started smiling and exclaimed in great joy how wonderful the fruit was and, *Mom, you really should try it!*

La, la, la, shookrun! I shook my head and I ran.

⁓

We had been in Cairo a couple of weeks and I'd been advised by one of the other ex-pat wives to buy my meat from The Fantastic Happy Dinner Man. I duly wrote my order, gave the piece of paper to Peter with instructions for Maha, his personal assistant to place the order as I had already tried, but the person at the other end of the phone couldn't speak English and my Arabic was still in its infancy. I could count to ten, say yes, no, please and thank you, come here and bugger off, but that was the sum total of my vocabulary. I doubted I could place an order for meat.

The doorbell rang. I opened it to find a slim Egyptian man with a beard and moustache standing in his stockinged feet in my entrance hall. He had a big grass basket hoisted onto his shoulders and I could smell the fresh meat in it.

"Ana Meesta Achmed, Fantastic Happy Dinner Man," he introduced himself.

I put out my hand to shake his in reciprocal greeting, but he backed off, nodding and bowing, a little like the Chinese do.

He swept past me, into the kitchen and banged the basket down on the floor. The cats, which had followed the scent of the fresh red meat, both shot up, their tails bushed out and they skedaddled out from under the feet of the man rushing around the kitchen. He took hold of the Sunlight liquid detergent which I'd brought from South Africa and washed down the marble counter tops of the kitchen unit. Then, delving down into the depths of his basket, Mr Achmed produced a wad of plastic bags and little white cards.

"Madame write, Meesta Achmed tell Madame what is".

I only worked out what he meant when he started packing the meat into portion controlled packets and telling me what each cut of meat was. I had to write this onto the little cards which he would then slip into the packet. Once this was done, Mr Achmed would pad across the kitchen and pack the meat into the deep freezer, rump and fillet at the top, chops on the middle shelf and lamb legs right at the bottom. I didn't buy fish as I was nervous it had been caught in the Nile... which was terribly dirty and I'm sure carried all types of diseases, running from its source in Ethiopia through Upper Egypt to the sewerage infested banks of the river in downtown Cairo.

Lastly, Mr Achmed would sanitize the kitchen sink—again using far too much of my precious Sunlight Liquid—and then write down the prices of each cut he had just packed into my freezer onto a large piece of paper. In Arabic.

I learnt to read Arabic numbers from the number plates on all the cars while driving through Cairo with Mohammed, Peter's driver. Mo couldn't speak English, I couldn't speak Arabic. But we got along just dandy using sign language. Being an artist, of sorts, I would keep a notepad handy and draw pictures which Mohammed would then translate. I do hope that *Agsakhana* really does mean pharmacy otherwise my sketching skills need to be revisited.

So learning to read numbers went something like this. Mo would point at the number plate on the car in front of us. He would lift one finger skywards and declare 'wahed'. So now I knew that the number one was 'wahed'. I would then teach him the English word for 'wahed' which he pronounced 'wwwohn'.

Came a particularly trying day when a tourist bus was blown up outside the Cairo museum. Traffic came to a standstill. Now if you've ever been to Egypt, you'll know that traffic does not have any form. Right of way belongs to the vehicle in front of you.

Robots work, but they are ignored. It's kamikaze stuff and you pray to G-d that you're going to make it home alive.

So there we were, stuck in a traffic jam.

"Mohammed," I asked, "*ma hoo'wa traffic jam fee elharda Arabie?*" Even if it was incorrectly said or pronounced, Mohammed understood. How do you say traffic jam in Arabic?

"Aaaah, Madame, Kabier Mashek." Which literally meant 'big problem'. So I then taught him the English version and years later, when driving friends or family who were visiting us, he would proudly point at the cars in the Cairene streets and exclaim, "N'raffic zham!"

Traffic jam. Didn't you understand?

One of the things I learnt to do (apart from playing a lousy game of golf) while living in Cairo, was the art of fabric painting. It was the late 1990's and the craze had taken over the South African creative crafting scene. My friend, Mariekie, the Major wife of the Colonel who was the Military Attaché at the South African Embassy, was just such a crafty woman.

Mariekie had brought buckets and buckets of paints in various colours and shades to Cairo, taking up any spare space they had in their 40 foot container of furniture and household goods.

She invited a group of ex-pat women around for coffee, cake and painting lessons one day. Mariekie was an incredibly good hostess—her tray cloths were painted to match the tea or coffee set she was serving from. Her table cloths were painted to match the theme of her dinners and lunches. I eagerly got stuck in to both the fabric painting... and the chocolate cake.

Before long, the two of us had a fabulous little industry going in the basement of my villa. We had imported paints from South Africa, the Egyptian cotton was perfect for painting on, and the

American school was asking us to produce goodies to sell at their annual Christmas Bazaar.

Early September, we got working. Five to six hours a day, we painted. We painted table cloths, tray cloths, cushion covers, tea cosies. If you could think of something for us to paint, we did.

Then we stitched up the stuff we painted. I had an old sewing machine, Mariekie had an overlocker. Together we stitched and overlocked our hand-painted stuff. I made labels on the computer and we were in business. The American women loved our wares. They bought tons and we made good money. The following year, the school contacted us in early January. Did we want to take a table at the Easter Bazaar? No thank you. We politely declined. We were fabric-painted out.

Now Mariekie was an Afrikaans-speaking South African while I had been schooled in a terribly proper British institution so my Afrikaans was as bad as her English was good. Ok, her English was worse. We started up our own pigeon Afrikaans-English. One day, during a painting session, I stretched back from bending over a table, having painted a border in one foul swoop with no stop for a breather.

"*Jislaak*, Mariekie, my back is *eina*," this meant to be spoken in Afrikaans.

"Wat's verkeerd met jou bek?" she asked, dabbing away at a huge piece of cloth she was painting. (What's the matter with your mouth?)

"Niks nie," I responded perplexed. (Nothing.)

"Maar jy se jou bek is seer?" she queried again, looking up at me curiously. (But you said your mouth was sore.)

"Nee man, I said my rug was seer". (No, man, I said my back was sore.)

In Afrikaans the word for mouth, *bek*, is pronounced similarly to the English word for back. At least we understood each other in all things crafting, even if not in our own languages.

Mariekie and I joined the expat craft club. I asked if Craft stood for Can't Remember A Fucking Thing. She said she couldn't remember.

One morning, we attended a session to make stained glass decals at Vanessa's apartment. Vanessa was the American wife of a French Naval Commander. She lived in the penthouse of an apartment block on the other side of the Nile in a suburb called Zamalek. Standing on the balcony drinking a cup of tea and having a smoke break, one of the Spanish women asked why Mariekie and I spoke in such different accents if we came from the same country.

"Well," I explained, "Mariekie is from the Afrikaaner speaking stock of South Africans, while I was brought up as an English speaking South African."

I continued to explain that South Africa now had eleven official languages.

"O la la," she exclaimed, "You can speak all these languages?"

Of course, that little red devil that lives on my right hand shoulder tugged at my ear and whispered... go on, tell her you can.

So I did. And she was so impressed, telling me that she struggled just to speak one additional language other than Spanish. I thought her English was particularly good. Better than my Xhosa or Zulu. And don't forget my Sepedi and Tswana. All of which were non-existent.

The following month, and feeling awful at having lied to this lady, I said to Mariekie as we were leaving to attend our craft club meeting, that I just had to confess I could not speak all eleven languages. I had trouble speaking the two I had learnt at school—and one was my mother tongue.

We arrived at our hostesses' apartment. The first thing I did was go looking for the Spanish Signora. But no matter where I looked, I just couldn't find her. Each time the doorbell rang and another expat lady walked in, I hoped it would be her. Alas, by the time we were having tea, she had still not arrived.

"Vanessa," I asked our hostess, "where is Carlotta today?"

"Ahhh," she shook her head sadly, "her husband passed away and she has returned to Spain."

"She is coming back, isn't she?" I urged, knowing already what her answer would be.

So, Carlotta, wherever you are, and you're telling people you met a South African woman in Egypt who could speak eleven languages, please don't tell them you just found out I lied.

It's A Technicolor World
I Live In, Misses Pat

*M*y life has always been about colour. I even dream in exploding hot diggity-dog technicolour. I ask you.

My mother always kept shaddup suckers in the glove compartment of my father's car. Shaddup suckers were exactly that. To get me to shut up when we were driving, especially on long distance trips, to visit our family 'up north'. I tended to (alright then, I still do) yak a lot.

Well understand this, whilst I had an elder brother and sister, they were already out of the house so to speak when I was born. My sister just going on sixteen, my brother even older. So to all intents and purposes, I was an only child.

Thus I had to keep myself company on those long trips. I think my chatting and singing and poetry recitals drove my parents scats. So I would be given a shaddup sucker almost as soon as we set off, gears grinding, shock absorbers groaning with the weight of the luggage piled high, not forgetting the *padkos* my Mom had packed.

Shaddup suckers were cellophane wrapped strips of lollipops

that came in robot colours. Red, orange and green. I didn't care for the orange ones and often had to do an *eenie meenie minie mo* between the red and green ones. Of course the red ones were my favourites. I would make sure there was loads of juicy spit in my mouth, picking up the red colour of the lollipop, which I would then rub all over my lips with my tongue. Well, a gal needs her lipstick doesn't she? And green lipstick wasn't fashionable back in the 60's.

If you ask me, I think red was my favourite colour as a young person.

My first bicycle was red. So was my first motorbike, and my first car was red too, come to think of it. Um, every car I've bought myself has been red. Does that tell you something? Psychiatrists and the like—put away your diagnoses and just go with the flow here please.

Whenever I give directions, I use colour as a reference. Like, turn left at the house with the turquoise garage doors. Heaven help us if the owners repaint their doors another colour without me knowing. Thank goodness for Google maps now. And GPS's... I've just found a BlackBerry app which is easy to use, gives directions in an English accent which I can understand. And yes, the screen is in... You guessed it... colour.

When my boys were young, their clothes were colour coded. New clothes, before they were even so much as put near a body, were run through the sewing machine with colour thread zigzagged on the inside labels. Red for Dane, green for Justyn, Wade loved blue and hello! (yellow) for Gregory, the little shit. That way we never had arguments about who owned what.

Peter will still to this day shout up the staircase "where'd you keep the roll of string?" and I'll reply "in the blue Tupperware box with the orange lid in the cupboard where the red tea-towels are kept". Colour again.

I am not, and have never been, scared of colour. Even my language, particularly when I'm miffed, becomes exceptionally colourful. The air can turn twelve different shades of blue when I lose the plot. That's when the kids and the cats feel the electricity in the air and they all run away.

As a child I loved getting Crayola as gifts. My Aunty Doreen, who was a real lady, was always the one to buy me the biggest set at Christmas time. I think the largest set I ever received was about 64 pieces—plus there were metallic bronze, silver and gold crayons in a separate bonus box. Those three would be savoured for the most splendid of pictures, usually adding bling (which did I mention I love?) to my artistic masterpieces. I would take the crayons out of their boxes, lay them out in their shades, from darkest to lightest, and would more often than not draw something which would include a rainbow or two. With the obligatory pot 'o gold coloured in, in metallic gold Crayola, right where it belonged. At the bottom of the rainbow.

Even today, with my machine embroidery, I have a chest of drawers holding many different colours of threads, all neatly arranged into shades, again from darkest to light, and in the format of a rainbow. Purples and pinks to reds, oranges and yellows, blues to greens not forgetting blacks, greys, whites, and metallics.

I love rainbows. All those colours together make my heart very happy. Fact, if I could get to the pot o' gold at the bottom of the rainbow I'd be even happier. Wouldn't we all. That a rainbow is formed because of various phenomena like refraction and reflection to produce a magical arc over my head is, in my mind, never short of a miracle.

And best of all... I live in a Rainbow Nation. How cool is that!

I'M GETTING MARRIED... IN LIME GREEN

We'd been living together for so many years that when friends asked Peter "when are you going to marry Trisch?" He would respond, "when I come back from Rio."

This would create great excitement in our circles. For one, South Africans didn't travel overseas that much in those days and if they did, it was cause for huge celebration. And two, it meant he'd finally come to his senses and was going to make an honest woman of me.

Naturally the next question would be "so when you going to Rio?" Upon which, Peter would get this dead-sucker thoughtful expression on his face, he'd put his forefinger on the left edge of his chin, tilt his head ever so slightly to the side, squint his eyes upwards and exclaim, "ummmm, never!"

It didn't pain me to hear this. In fact, I would be the one whoop-whooping and laughing just as loud as the next. I had, years previously, made an amazing pact with myself about the marriage thing. I had already been down the aisle once and wasn't over-enamoured with the idea of hitching myself to another man who would, I thought, strip me of my identity which I had struggled to reinvent after a nasty divorce. My business was booming, I had bought myself a house, a car and a whole bunch of debt so why did I need a man to help add to all of that?

Peter too had gone through an acrimonious divorce and wasn't keen to get hitched again. In fact, he was downright forthright about it.

One cold winters evening, Peter and I were lying on the floor in the formal lounge in front of a roaring fire. We were playing Rummy, which he always beat me at, and drinking Southern Comfort on the rocks.

"Trischa," he said, "there are three things I will never do. One, I will never tell you I love you. Two, I will never buy you jewellery, and three, I will never marry you."

Liar, liar, your pants are still on fire.

At the time, however, I had two choices - and they were both bad. I could fight for the ring and the wedded bliss and lose him completely. Or I could accept my lot, buy my own jewellery, be happy with his terms of endearments like "of course I like you, what's not to like?" and have the man in my life. No choice. I went out and bought myself the most beautiful ring and slipped it on my right hand as a reminder that this was a promise ring... a promise that I would never trap him into anything he didn't want to be trapped into.

So one Thursday evening, about seven years into 'living in sin' which Peter's mother just couldn't handle... ouch, there's another chapter there I tell you... I kick my shoes off at the front door and pad through in my stockinged feet to the kitchen, where the cats are already meowing their indignation at being fed so late. Mozart and Chopin are demanding their evening meal, snaking through my legs and making such a noise I can't hear myself think.

"Ok, Ok, in a minute, patience," I tell them, dropping a kiss on Peter's forehead as he sits at the table reading the latest Scope magazine.

As I get the Friskies out, Peter mumbles from behind his magazine (come to think of it, it might actually have been the Garden and Home), "whatcha doin' on Tuesday?"

"Um, I have two appointments, one with Hyperama and the other with Plascon."

"Cancel 'em."

"Why?"

"Coz we're getting married."

"Yeah, right, ha ha," I laughed as I went about feeding the kitties. I wondered if he was going to Rio again. But I chortled good naturedly about it, started making dinner and eventually forgot the conversation. Until the following Monday morning.

"Meet me outside," Peter bellowed over the telephone line.

He was phoning from his car phone and the line wasn't all that good. This was in the days just before cell phone technology had been introduced into South Africa. If you had a car phone you were considered very fortunate and obviously one of the elite. Which neither of us was. We were just lucky that someone had owed Peter money and repaid it in the form of a car phone kit.

"What must I meet you outside for?" I asked.

I had a dozen job cards to get sorted and hadn't even had my first cup of coffee for the day.

"We need to go into Jo'burg City. I'll fetch you in about five minutes."

"What for?" I asked again.

Sometimes being blonde isn't all from the bottle. But at the time I really had no idea what the man was talking about. I shuffled the job book to one side, picked up a pile of invoices and stapled them together.

"We need to get copies of our divorce papers; otherwise we can't get married tomorrow."

"Are you *serious?*"

My heart nearly stopped beating, suddenly I was hyperventilating, my hands got all clammy, and I burst into tears. My secretary ran into my office, bearing tissues and far too much sympathy which just got those tear ducts working even harder.

Once I'd calmed down, once we'd got the copies of our divorce papers, once Peter had dropped me back off at my office, I suddenly did the back of hand on forehead oh-my-gawd-I've-got-nothing-to-wear-to-get-married-in thing. Which saw me scurrying off to an haute couture boutique in Sandton City and spending an obscene amount of money on a wedding outfit. If that's what you could call it.

The saleslady looked at me a little bit squiffy, then she saw the cubics on my fingers and in my ears, thought the shoes might have been Jimmy Choo's, but then they could have been Bally, and stepped forward, very similar to the infamous scene in Pretty Woman where Julia Roberts goes shopping on Rodeo Drive. Just for the record, I did not look like Julia Roberts shopping on Rodeo Drive in that awful blue thing called a dress wearing cock-sucker boots. But I do wish I'd had the body that she put in it.

"Um," I said rather shyly, "I'm getting married tomorrow and I've got nothing to wear."

The sales lady put her hand in the small of my back, and in a very conspiratorial whisper as she propelled me towards the racks, said, "Shall we look at whites or perhaps another colour would be more suitable?"

I was so dim I didn't realize until years later that she probably thought it was a shotgun wedding and that I was pregnant.

As I said before, those were the 80's. Dallas and Dynasty were big hits on South African television, with Linda Grey and Joan

Collins making padded shoulders very fashionable and an absolute requirement for every unexpectedly-soon-to-be-married, like-in-tomorrow, bride's outfit. It was my dream come true. It was just perfect. It was also ridiculously expensive, but I didn't give a fig. Or a peach, or a plum. I was getting married in the morning. The saleslady tried very hard to sell me the matching hat. I refused, but I did capitulate and buy the matching ear-rings.

Ka-Ching!

So that was how I came to be married, in the magistrate's courts above a bakery in Kempton Park on a cold August morning, in a lime green power suit, complete with black military-style detail on the cuffs and collar, the most wonderfully wide shoulder pads and black stockings and shoes.

Perfect for a bride.

CHROME IS THE COLOUR OF
MY TRUE LOVE'S HARLEY

Peter sent Dane an email with a photograph attached of his new silver Mercedes SLK 320 something-or-the-other parked in the driveway. Dane was living the in the USA at the time. He wrote in an email to me—'Ma, has my father had a midlife crisis?'

Silly boy, of course not. Your father's only 45 years old. Midlife what?

A couple of years later, we collected Dane at the airport. He'd come home to finally try and get his Visa issues sorted out. You know the Americans, you can't do it there... you have to come back to what they consider to be a third world country, for G-d's sake, to get your work visa right from their very own consulate! But that we'll devote another chapter to later on.

So there we are, one cold August morning. No, not a hot August night, this is the southern hemisphere and it's *vrek* cold in the mornings on the Highveld. We've ridden the new Gautrain, and then caught the bus to a depot near our house. While this is

79

the normal form of transport in many countries, South Africa still doesn't have a public transport system and it is sorely needed. Without such we are forced to own motor vehicles. Hence the traffic problems and grid-lock we face on a daily basis to-ing and fro-ing down the highways to our places of work.

We pull up to the garage doors at the side of our house. Peter flicks the remote control and both wooden doors roll up. On the left hand side sits said cute little SLK (now renamed the SL-Gay). On the right hand side are not one, but two Harley-Davidson motorbikes. Big, beautiful, all black and chrome, mean looking mother-fuckers. Dane does a little double take, just a little one, and in all seriousness says to us, "You know, Ma, when I joked that Peter had had a midlife crises I really thought it was just a joke. But now I see it's confirmed. You've both had one!"

The boy has a sense of humour.

Two days later we're riding off to a breakfast in the Magaliesberg and Dane's shouting from behind Peter, "faaaarrrrk, Ma, this is awesome!"

None of my other kids have Harleys. Thank goodness.

Wade, however, has all types of every other kind of bike under the sun, but none of them are strictly street-going. He packs his camel-pack with OJ and buzzes off on a Sunday morning to some dreadful dirty donga-riddled track where other such people gather. They all then race off together, skidding the soles of their feet along the road, trying to make as big a cloud of dust as possible. Now I understand where the expression *eat my dust* comes from.

Wade does this all day, then gets home, showers and goes off to visit his girlfriend where he promptly falls asleep on the couch and leaves her feeling quite ignored and as grumpy as all hell. He puts it down to PMT; I put it down to no nookies. When will these kids ever learn?

Neither Justyn nor Gregory have ever ridden a motorbike, never mind been on one. They are city-slickers who do the car thing.

Dane has Miss Muriel.

My colleagues at work think I have a split-personality disorder. During office hours, I am demurely dressed, no décolletage showing, my feet always well shod and my hair and makeup just so. My fragrance is subdued and I wear rimless reading glasses. I carry a Polo handbag which has my Mont Blanc pen set in its leather holder nestled in one of the side compartments for easy access. My iPad and mobile are synced; my laptop is pink. I am a career woman of note.

But when work's out, I slap on my leathers, paint my nails hectic pink, pencil my eyelids with turquoise eyeliner, bling up my belt buckles, wrap leather armbands around my wrists and I ride, Sally, I ride!

One year for my birthday, Peter bought me a beautiful leather set to wear during the cold winter months. He had it imported from Harley in the USA. The pants are padded at thigh, knee and hip. They have zippers down the sides which reveal bright orange inners. The jacket sports a built-in kidney belt. It has more pockets in it than my mother's old handbag had, and that had some. There is space to keep everything from your iPod to your iPhone on your body, complete with a cloth to clean your spectacles or visor suspended inside a pocket on an elasticised string.

The set is made by Harley-Davidson FXRG. I don't know what FXRG really stands for, but in my language it means Fucking Expensive Riding Gear.

WHY'S IT CALLED THE RED SEA
WHEN IT'S TURQUOISE?

Sharm el Sheikh on the Red Sea was our six-weekly weekend time-out spot. We tried to get out of Cairo every six weeks, away from the smog and the dirt, the unhygienic conditions that existed outside the villa we lived in, and the incessant irritation of the donkey-cart drivers and the *boabs* (security men/caretakers/ doormen) shouting at each other, their habibi music blaring from the TV's and the 'whallah... Allie's snack bar' being yodelled from the minarets every hour, on the hour.

There's a blogger on the internet who sums up the Egyptian Boabs like this.

"Having a boab in Egypt is like having your 8 year old brother stand out in front of your room (24hrs a day), judge your guests, comment on your life choices, kiss your ass like it's never been kissed before, and ask for a quarter because he polished your doorknob by virtue of him turning it to let the plumber in. I thought that my boabs were particularly intrusive, but found out later that it is the norm. At 3 a.m., my boab rolls a bed out into the lobby and sleeps there. There's no way to come home without waking him up, and when you do, the drama starts. "Oh, I was sleeping, but that's okay, ya Pasha!"

I couldn't have put it better.

We went snorkelling in the Red Sea. All the other S'Africans in Egypt learnt to scuba dive while living there. We didn't. Firstly, we felt the kids were too young to be allowed to scuba and secondly I am so *vrek* scared of the water and don't think I would manage having to suck on a pipe to take in oxygen. I am convinced I drowned in a previous life and that is why I just don't do water. Or swimming, or surfing, or any sport remotely connected to that stuff that covers 70% of the earth's surface. The fact that Peter even got me to *consider* snorkelling was an amazing feat worthy of a Nobel Prize for Persistence.

The night before our first trip to the Red Sea was filled with silly antics in the dining room of Villa 49. We had been to the Alpha Market, our local one-stop shop, to buy snorkelling gear. The boys were buggering around trying on their new flippers and masks. I was in fits of laughter at them, the tears rolling down my face. Peter and Dane, when they get onto the same track, become the funniest duo. The one starts, the other continues, and around and around they go, each quip or motion funnier than the last. I still have the photo of them in my album... it's aptly titled 'A bunch of goofy footed fattypoeses!'

Welcome on board Egypt Scare, internationally known as Egypt Air. The flight to Sharm el Sheikh is only about an hour, but in that hour I've prayed that Hashem will take us quickly and painlessly if the plane is a) blown up by fundamentalists/terrorists, b) loses a very important screw which keeps the engine from falling off the wing or c) that the smell in the cabin doesn't asphyxiate us.

I almost kiss the ground as we deplane, but the smell of

the tarmac on that hot summers' morning is enough to turn my stomach. I don't do smells. My family laugh at me, but my schnoz can smell a dead camel thirty miles away and the wind doesn't even have to be blowing in my direction. I heave when I'm confronted with nasty smells. That's why, when my kids were babies and needed nappy changes, I handed them, while trying not to puke, over to their nannies. That's also why I pressed a hanky with lavender oil to my nostrils during that particular plane ride (and many subsequent ones). And I took a valium to still my nerves.

Fortunately, the hotel we book into is good and clean and fresh tra-la-la.

It's amazing what one remembers from one's childhood. A TV advert in the 1980's had a really catchy jingle… it's good and clean and fresh tra-la-la… which we all still sing to this day when we've just had a shower, washed our hair, tumble dried our towels or cleaned the house, even though the advert was originally for washing powder. I think.

We leave the cool confines of our clean hotel and saunter down to the jetty where an impressive yacht is moored. We've hired it for the day. Both Peter and I don't do sharing-with-strangers so easily, so we've taken a look at all the tourists clambering aboard the other boats in the bay and found a yacht which doesn't seem to be filled with all types of everybody. I'm sorry, but I have no desire to have strange foreign men drooling over me as I lie in my itsy-bitsy yellow polka dotted bikini while the men in my life submerge themselves in the nether regions of the coral reef to spot fish.

The boys are happily lugging our masks and flippers along. I have grabbed the hotel's beach towels and Peter has his camera at the ready. We get onto the yacht and, at the finger pointing of the skipper who's English is non-existent, we read "Please Shoese

Off". Shoese off yourself, mate. We take our *plakkies* off and make ourselves comfortable in the cabin.

For roughly an hour, we sail across the Red Sea, which is actually the most incredible turquoise I have ever seen, finally coming to anchor at a small bay. The sand is a dull brown and I see no trees or palms swaying in the breeze.

"Don't be daft, Trisch," Peter laughs, "we're in the middle of the fucking desert, there are no palms here, it's not Durban!"

The dive master, Yachyer, instructs the boys on the hand signals he will use as they snorkel around the bay. I prefer to stay closer to the yacht, wallowing in the warm salty water whilst hanging on to a guide rope securely fastened to the back of the boat.

"Mom!" says Dane excitedly as they get back to the yacht, "we saw a parrot fish!"

"Me too." I answer.

"And we saw a stingray!" chirps Justyn.

"So did I."

"Did you see the turtle as well then?" asks Peter, almost disbelievingly.

"You mean that one?"

I point at a turtle moseying past us, lazily making his way who knows where. He lifts his head slightly out of the water and I swear he winked at me.

While I hadn't snorkelled with the guys that day, I saw just about everything they did. I'd gotten bored sitting watching dull dusty desert scenery from the deck and so had very gingerly put on my mask and breathing tube, made my way slowly into the water behind the yacht and, while hanging on tightly to the rope, I'd put my head cautiously under the water.

I got such a fright. I heard my own breathing and nearly jumped right back into the yacht. But I put my head under again and before long I was floating in the Red Sea, watching the underwater parades of angel and clown fish, jellyfish and little zebra looking dudes as they all went their merry way.

I must say, the Red Sea never quite got me over my fear of water, but throughout the following years in Egypt, I never missed an opportunity to snorkel with the guys, marvelling at the beautiful coral and the never-ending array of brightly coloured fish.

And I never even had to learn to scuba.

Die Pienk Dame

I t's oppressively hot under my helmet. My brain feels like it's been par-boiled. 41degC at midday in the middle of the Karoo and it seems like we're so far off the beaten track I fear we might not see civilization again in my lifetime.

Talking which, I almost shorten said lifetime by hitting a nasty pothole on the first bend in the poort we've just entered. I find myself flying through the air, Harley going one way, me the other. Stars appear before my eyes, as do the faces of each of my children as well as that of my beloved husband who has disappeared around the second bend ahead of me, blissfully unaware of my encounter with the Karoo tar.

The first thought that enters my head as I roll to a halt is to get the hell off the tar and onto the gravel—you know, just in case a big truck comes around the corner and finishes me off. Not that we've seen a truck, let alone any other vehicle on the road for more than an hour. I hobble to the side of the road and sit down in the tall dry brown veld grass. I feel a bit woozy so I lie down. Then I sit bolt upright as my addled brain starts thinking of rattle snakes and some such other critters slithering over my lifeless body. By the way, we don't get rattlesnakes in South Africa. I finally hear the thumpa thumpa of a Harley engine in the distance. My knight in shining and heavily chromed armour has arrived to rescue me. The darling man leans over his handle bars and queries, "What happened?"

"I fricking fell off, didn't I?" I spit out. Oh that nasty snake has got my tongue.

Dead silence in the Karoo hurts your ears. Not a breath of wind to break the quiet. Not a blade of grass stirs. Even the birds have buggered off to cooler climes. I lie down and all I hear is a doef-doef in my head. Oh hell, I've still got my earphones in and my MP3 player is thundering soft rock into my bejiggled cranial matter. I could do with real soft rock... the tar is quite hard on my left hip.

Peter whips out the Dis-Chem first aid kit, wields the scissors with the skill of a diesel mechanic about to attempt micro-surgery, slices away at my new jeans, tossing them over the side of the embankment and tourniquets my lacerated knee with every possible bandage he can find in the limited kit.

"How far are we from the next town?" I ask.

"About thirty kilometers," he answers, struggling to stop the flow of blood spurting from my knee.

"I'm ok you know, I can ride to the next town and then we can find a doctor there. I think I'll need some stitches."

Some might think I'm a brave girl. Others have every right to disagree. I will stay perched on the fence on this one. Put it down to adrenaline.

So I stand up. Peter has managed to get my bike up onto its stand. It looks like all is okay except the headlight is gone and the speedometer which once was encased with Swarovski crystals (I told you I love bling) has disappeared over the side of the mountain too.

I get on the bike, feeling quite confident.

"I can't pull in the clutch," I say, "run next to me and let the clutch out slowly while I accelerate and I can put-put down to the next town."

I fire up my bike. She sounds okay. Just a weird petrol smell around, but then that's to be expected I suppose. Peter lifts the side stand with his foot, I accelerate and he lets out the clutch slowly while running next to me. I wobble. Then I fall off again.

Just at this moment a little car arrives with two very young people peering nervously over the dashboard and ask with a quiver in their voices if we need help. Do we ever?

Fearing my brain is bleeding, I get into the front seat of the little car with helmet still on head. I figure I've watched far too much ER on TV—there is no way anyone other than a surgeon will remove it from my nut. The car is packed to the hilt with suitcases, pillows, blankets and boxes of fruit. The young lady helps me into the front seat which cannot go back at all due to the stuff shoved in behind it. My legs are a bit longer than hers, so I have to bend my already damaged knee so much I fear the wound will tear even more and I'll bleed to death.

Seems like the couple had just left a hotel near Steytlerville where their uncle worked as the Manager. This, they decide, is the best place to take me as they know there is no doctor, pharmacy or hospital in the little town. *Oom* Jacques will know exactly what to do, they assure us.

Peter and the young man are left behind to try pick up the pieces and move my gear onto Peter's bike. He will follow on down to the hotel once the young man is picked up and the couple carry on along their way.

Ensconced in the safe cocoon of the car's interior, we zigzag through the poort to one quaint establishment called the Karroo Theatrical Hotel. One kilometre of dust road later and my lady driver is still looking worriedly at me. Not because I was about to vomit, you understand, but I think she was panicking about her beautiful new clean car and the blood dripping from the bandages around my leg. Skidding to a halt, she pulled the little car up to the front gate, hopped out and scurried around to open the door.

Enter, centre stage, one Pink Lady.

The car door opens. I dip my head to climb out and am surprised to see a pair of male feet with nails painted the most fabulous shade of pink standing next to the car door. Looking up I'm met by ginormous hands reaching out to help me - also painted with that same fabulous shade of *binnepoes-pienk*. Then a resonant tenor voice (I swear I thought it was an angel and I was either already dead or on my way to being dead) asks me, "Can you walk?"

"Nah-ah," I manage, "can you carry me?"

"*Liewe arde, nee!*" he responds, shouting over my head, "*Markie kom help my met die biker dame met die rooi naels!*" (Dear heavens, no! Marky, come help me with the biker lady with the red nails!")

Jacques is just over six foot tall with the physique of a body builder. He has the most exquisitely sculpted eyebrows. His skin is tanned golden, his legs are shaven clean. I see a hint of powder on his nose. He also has a torso to die for girls, but alas, he's most definitely a nine Rand note. In other words, girls, he just doesn't do girls. Period. Er, full stop.

With his help, I make it onto the couch on the *stoep*. Jacques goes in search of ice and a cold drink for me.

A couple of moggy kitties and a multi-coloured rooster eye me out. I cock an eye at them too. Jacques brings me a towel filled with ice from the bar and plonks it onto my lacerated knee.

The table is drawn near and my leg is lifted gently by those huge hands to rest on the table. I sit hugging the ice under my chin, still with my helmet on, hoping the coolness will bring my core temperature down from *blerrie* hot to just manageable before I expire out in the middle of nowhere.

Two litres of Coke later, I tentatively feel around the edges of my helmet. I can't feel anything dripping out so I take it off. Relief. I feel safe. I drift off to sleep for a while...

Two months later to the day I ride up that same dust road, this time I get off a Harley and walk onto the *stoep* of the Karroo Theatrical Hotel healthy and without help. There's a slight limp to the one side and a bit of a wiggle to the other. My knee doesn't look pretty anymore. My collarbone juts out a bit.

But I am alive and well and back in the saddle... and I'm in Steyterville, comparing nail polish colours with my Pink Lady.

GREEN AND GOLD—GO BOKKE!

N ow I, for one, can't tell the difference between my John Smits and my Jonty Rhodes. In fact, even when they're on the field in their respective team gear, I still can't tell one from the other except that the guy with the red hair is a cricketer. I think.

I'm quite the source of amusement (and often embarrassment) to my sports-mad husband. He is a typical South African male. Come weekends, he ensconces himself in front of the TV in the lounge, remote control in hand and switches channels as deftly as a woman changing her mind. Quite easily and quite frequently.

He also shouts at the referees (as all South African sports mad males do) most often exclaiming, with one hand on the head, the other palm up with one finger pointing accusingly at the offending player, "aw c'mon ref, that was a knock on." Then, when the referee hasn't stopped to walk over and peer out of the TV and say, "oh dear, you're quite right, Peter," he'll slump back on the couch where the kitty has just settled in for an afternoon nap, causing said kitty to yirouw, spit, claw and jump on top of him, sending the beer he's just picked up spilling all over my beautiful Iranian silk carpet.

Peter has a couple of sports-mad pals who frequently make their way up to our house to watch important matches on our large TV. Again, I'm not sure why these matches are so important. It's just a game, guys... isn't it?

One of these mad friends is a gregarious fellow who I originally met though a business deal I put together. Fränzo is of Afrikaans and German stock. He's as pedantic as the Germans and as full of shit as the Afrikaners. What a combination. He's one of the few people I know who still collects vinyl, for G-ds' sake. He's a wealth of knowledge on local music and supports bands with peculiar names like *Beeskraal* (Cattle Enclosure) and *Fokof Polisie Kar*. I think you got that one.

Fränzo brings home-made beef soup for the winter rugby matches. I make the bread. Peter and I have travelled many miles together with Fränzo, to rugby games, near and far, always supporting our *Bokke* wearing our Green and Gold proudly, our backpacks filled with Jagermeister and *biltong*. And he has a wonderfully loud and infectious laugh. If ever you need a pick me up, phone 0800-Fränzo.

One international game we went to with Fränzo and his colleague Carel, was in Port Elizabeth. The *Bokkies* were playing against the All Blacks. It was a riotous afternoon that we had, shared with the MD of a prestigious wine club who thoroughly enjoyed six quarts of beer in the first half. The Bokkies annihilated those Kiwi's.

We continued our carousing way into the early hours of the morning at a local restaurant, eating freshly shucked oysters, grilled prawns and South Africa's famous malva pudding, a sticky baked gingery pudding which is soaked with apricot jam. And then just for good measure, a big dollop of yellowy-orange custard splurged over the top. Makes my mouth water just writing about it. You too?

At 5.30am, we were up and about, ready to make the gruelling trip from PE to East London to catch a flight home from there. Tickets back from PE were like trying to find hens teeth and Carel's secretary had done her best to ensure we all got home on the Sunday afternoon.

Packing our gear, I noticed eight pockets of oranges in the boot of the rental car.

"What's this?" I blearily ask Carel. Wishing for a glass of fresh fruit juice to clear my *na-dors* had been in my thoughts. But having to physically cut and squeeze the oranges wasn't exactly what I had in mind.

"My father-in-law brought us each two pockets of Patensie oranges this morning," he answered, "they are the best you'll ever taste."

You have to be kidding. We're going to get on an aeroplane with a backpack holding our overnight gear and two pockets of oranges, one under each arm? Yip. That is exactly what we are each going to do.

It was quiet in the car as we drove up the coastal road towards East London. Nursing hangovers of note and suffering from a lack of sleep, we'd all been keeping pretty much to ourselves, with an occasional quip here and there. Fränzo had connected his iPod into the car's stereo system. It was playing some soft Afrikaans rock music. Carel was snacking on dried apricots which smelled like a teenage schoolboy's grey wool socks.

We drove through King Williams Town. On the banks of the Buffalo River, King Williams Town was originally started as a mission station. Its once tree-lined streets were now bare, the wood having been used for fires. There was no green grass on the pavements. Outer walls in dire need of a coat of paint still had traces of the retailers names painted over the doorways.

We morosely looked out of the cars windows at the shambles of a town, once the hub of the area's agricultural and commercial centre.

"You know what?" Peter broke the silence.

"What?" Fränzo turned around in his seat.

We all waited for a pearl of wisdom.

"This place is fucked." said Peter, very matter-of-factly.

While living in Cairo, we were fortunate enough to have South African pay TV services. This kept Peter (and many other South African expat men) very happy as they could watch their favourite sport on TV in a language they could understand. Egyptians don't do rugby. They play soccer. And their TV stations should go back onto the Ark and preferably drown this time around.

Of particular note in our rugby-viewing annuls are Allen and Ina, a great couple with great children and a great passion for rugby. One is Australian, the other South African and this is, in sports terms, a partnership made in hell. Since hell froze over, Aussies and S'Africans have had a war on, both on rugby fields and cricket pitches. When there's an important game being played, one would arrive at our house decked out in yellow and green, the other in green and gold, *nogal* waving a flag and with our rainbow flag painted on her cheek.

They would settle in for the ninety minutes, munching happily on the *biltong* I'd made and swigging copious amounts of Castle Lager (in those days, South Africa's most-consumed beer).

Now, Mr Fantastic Happy Dinner Man's prices on sirloin and rump were rather prohibitive. Especially for making South

Africa's national snack. Cured and dried meat. Biltong. And no, it is absolutely nothing like jerky.

Instead, I would go up to Kimo Market where a side of beef, probably water buffalo, would cost me next to nothing. I would prepare the meat, pickling and spicing it with my secret recipe, then hang it from a clothes rack in the spare bedroom, the air conditioner set to aerate the room and keep the meat from going miffy. This would drive the cats crazy. Mozart was even found walking along the edge of the balcony between bedrooms on the first floor of the villa in his quest to track down the delicious aroma of the drying delicacy.

One tri-nations rugby final, the South Africans were up against the Australians. Again. Allen and Ina were, as usual, at our house to watch the game. The TV lounge was decked with South African flags and Bokkie paraphernalia.

Ina and Peter start the ragging with Allen, ganging up against him, teasing him, ribbing him, making him puff up and proudly assert "hundred bucks says you guys are going to lose."

Poor guy takes it square on the chin like a good Aussie when he hands over the dosh.

I sit on the fence, not wanting to upset either of them for I know, when these two countries battle it out on the rugby field, one of my friends is going home grumpy and guaranteed of no nooky that night.

I want no part of it.

One year we were persuaded by another proud Bok supporter friend to join a group of equally proud Bok supporter friends on a tour to Scotland and England.

At the time, we were living in Switzerland, so we flew in to Edinburgh and met up with them there. The tour group had witnessed the first of three games, being the one between the South African and Welsh teams in Cardiff, so they were already on a high. We eagerly joined in, having been miserable for six rainy weeks in Zurich and in sore need of some local home-grown camaraderie.

Came the day of the big game. We walked through the historic city of Edinburgh, the castle rising above the crowds en-route to the stadium. The roads had literally been closed to allow supporters to make their way to Murrayfield. This was one of Peter's biggest dreams. To be at a game in such a prestigious venue. He was walking on air through the streets of Edinburgh, singing Afrikaans songs like "*hier kom die Allie-bama, die Allie-bama, hy kom oor die see.*" Which has absolutely nothing to do with rugby.

But when you're a South African, and you're far away from home, despite being an English speaking South African, for some obscure reason, you resort to speaking Afrikaans and singing songs which you only know because you were forced to learn them at school.

That day, we walked past Scots in their kilts with pipers and drummers piping and drumming us in to the stadium, the green and gold supporters singing "*jou kombers en my matrass, en daar le die ding.*"

And displayed on the big screens outside the stadium was a S'Efriken supporter holding a cardboard banner proclaiming "Ma, tape die dronk ek's rugby." (Ma, tape the drunk I'm rugby.)

South Africans living in Scotland were cashing in on the tourists. They had bags of biltong for sale along the route. At ten British Pounds a bag, they were making enough money to see them through the rest of the year, I'm certain, considering it probably only cost them a Pound for what they were selling.

Our Spingbok team were playing the Scots, so it was a sea of navy blue supporters versus the green and golds. Peter was decked out in his gear, I hadn't packed any in. In retrospect, maybe that's because in those days I wasn't as avid a supporter as I am now and probably had scoffed at the idea of spending a lot of money on a jersey I would only wear occasionally. If only I would listen to my own reason. In the years since, I have collected an impressive wardrobe of *Ama-Bokke-Bokke* gear.

But that Saturday, in the freezing cold of Murrayfield stadium, I stuck out like a sore thumb in my thermally-insulated, not-so-subtle, bright red jacket.

Peter is still convinced that I was the cause of the 53-3 loss.

Sing Altogether Now... Red, Red Wine

B ob Marley must have visited South Africa in order to make his song Red, Red Wine such a hit. I can't remember an occasion when we've been a bit *poeg-eyed* on some of South Africa's best where some idiot hasn't starting singing it. Usually it's me.

You might think I'm biased, but I have tasted wines from many countries and when given the choice of the best French, or South African plonk, I settle for home-made plonk. Not only does it suit my pocket, but one thing I've worked out, SA's plonk is as good as, if not better, than some wines making the 2012 forbes. com top international wines list. And what we think of as plonk here in South Africa, is often featured in hotels around the globe as imported wine, costing you an arm and a leg.

Peter and I had decided to take a trip down to the south of Holland to a wonderful old castle which had been converted into a hotel. The original turret hosts the hotels two suites, one above the other. We booked into the first floor suite on this particular trip.

Both coming from Dutch heritage, we embrace the culture, enjoying cheese, pickled eel, *haring* and *poffertjes*. In fact, I've even made traditional *ertje sop* (pea soup) complete with pigs ear, trotter and *rook worst* where the soup becomes so thick a spoon can stand up alone in it. This soup, on a cold winters night, warms the cockles of your heart... oh hang on, Patricia, that's Irish chowder... anyway, you get the drift, *ertje sop* warms you up, makes you feel all fuzzy and happy and loving life.

So where do soup and red wine tie up you're asking? Well, there we were, in this delightful old castle in the south of Holland, eating pea soup out of the most exquisite white tableware, sitting in the dungeon which hosted bottles and bottles of old wines nestled into racks along the walls.

The waiter offers the wine menu to Peter. I see him scan down the page, then he turns it, and he scans down the next page. By the time he's scanned a few more pages my curiosity is just about bursting right out of my skin. For goodness sake, share your opinion with me, I silently urge him, not wanting to look like a complete palooka in front of the waiter. Who was quite cute. Peter leans towards him and asks for a bottle of Nederberg Cabernet.

Nederberg Cabernet Sauvignon, irrespective of the vintage, is a medium-bodied South African red wine, one which is not only in the upper price range, but, in those late 1990's, was often sold out as soon as it hit the shelves. It's mature deep red colour and smoky claret-type nose, with hints of berries, vanilla-oak and cassis is a perfect accompaniment to most roasted and braised red meat dishes.

"What are we celebrating?" I ask, thinking his choice is going to cost us dearly, so best it be put to good use.

"Just being here, and enjoying life." He answers smugly.

"Okay, spill the beans, *bekam*?" I resort to the Arabic word meaning 'how much'?

The waiter appears at the table and presents the bottle to

Peter for inspection. He nods his approval and the waiter grandly pours the liquid into clear large bulbous wine glasses. We savour the perfectly balanced taste, which leaves a silky long juicy finish on our palates. Ha. You think I'm a wine connoisseur, do you? Not by a long shot. I just read John Platters Wine Guide every time Peter and I try a new wine so that when I need to impress, like now, I can spew forth with great ease and really sound like I know what I'm talking about.

That wonderfully cold February evening, we feasted on the most beautiful casserole of beef with vegetables grown right in the castle grounds. Peter ordered a second bottle of Cab which went down just as smoothly as the first. I was convinced by now he'd either won the lottery or was spending our dosh like a mad-man because he knew the end of the world was nigh. Even the Mayans got it wrong, Peter.

Like most Dutchmen, we finished off our meal with a vanilla ice-cream. Sitting comfortably in the wing-back chairs in the dining room of the hotel, satiated beyond belief, Peter eventually confessed to the cost of the wine.

It was cheaper in Holland—and in a hotel, *nogal* - than it was in South Africa. *Keh*? I still want to send a note one day to Nederberg and ask them why. Why send our local produce overseas for people who probably have no clue about its nose and your palate, and who probably would eat it with fish and chips too. Sacrilegious! *Sacre Bleu!*

Which brings me to the French.

SACRE BLEU! ALL FRENCH ARE POUSSEZS

I call the French poesays. That's because they are. Both in terms of the Afrikaans description of *poes*, and in the French *poussez*—which means push—which they are. Pushy.

During early 1997, Peter and I sat around the dining room table of our home in Johannesburg, South Africa and asked our children how they would feel about leaving our mother country and moving to Egypt. We had already been on a look-see in late March. Peter's career was taking off with Coca-Cola and they had offered him an awesome opportunity within their ex-pat system.

After viewing the American International School's campus in Maadi, Cairo, I felt we could give our children so much more through being schooled there rather than in the crumbling South African government education system. Quite frankly, at that stage we couldn't afford the crippling costs of a private school for the boys either.

Gregory of course was too little to make any kind of decision, and, as he was living with his mother, we also knew he would not be able to come with us when we initially spoke to the kids about the move. Despite trying, we got a bit of a backhander from his mother which meant the little shit wouldn't have the same opportunities as the two boys who lived with us permanently. Ditto for Wade. His father just flat out refused to even consider the possibility that he would have an adventure par excellence.

This saddened me, but in the interests of not putting our kids in the middle and tugging at them from both directions, both Peter and I acquiesced to our respective ex-spouses and vowed that we would still show the kids what the world was made of. If not through living with us, then at least through holidaying with us around the world.

So with Dane and Justyn's permissions, we started the Great Trek north. Listen, with the amount of shit we'd accumulated through our lives by that stage, an *ossewa* wouldn't have been big enough, so we enlisted the services of a company who was proudly South African and *ama*-zing.

Peter flew up to Egypt a month ahead of us. I spent that month trying to sell the house, pack up, get rid of, buy new, sort out finances, obtain tax clearance certificates and so on and so on. The boys loved it because I kept them out of school. What was the point? They were going off to Cairo American College and would start the same grades all over again in the September.

One week before departure, a loyal client phoned me. He had a last favour to ask before I left our borders. Would I, could I, pretty please with bells and whistles on the top, do just one last design job for him? My brain went into calculator mode. I didn't really want to be bogged down with design at this point, but if I over-quoted and he accepted, then I'd use the money to take the boys on a proper holiday before landing in Egypt. Disney Paris, I thought. I quoted and the client accepted. I designed. Then I bought a trip to Egypt via France.

We boarded Air France in the early evening. The tears had already dried up before we'd gone through passport control. I'd told the boys that I'd arranged for seats in the bubble of the Jumbo Jet. This excited them and they promptly forgot about their cousins lamenting back in the departures hall at not being able to visit as frequently as they used to. The few members of Peter's family, my niece and sister-in-law and my friend Ian were already a distant memory as we waved our final farewells to them at Jan Smuts Airport.

Once we landed at Charles de Gaulle, we rushed to the car rental company to pick up our hire car. I looked at the little Renault Clio in amazement. It was so small there was absolutely no way I was going to pack 2 kids, 5 suitcases, a boombox and all our roll-on cabin bags into it without leaving space for me to drive. The French lady at the counter was quite disdainful when I went back to her to ask for a bigger car. At no extra cost, *s'il vous plaît*. I lost that round, so off we went, whizzing through the streets of Paris in a little green *gat gogga*, to the Hilton Hotel where we were booked in for a few nights. En-route, I turned to Justyn who was an avid drinker of water, and said, "listen, kid, you don't touch the taps here okay? You want water, I buy it for you in a bottle."

All fresh from a quick shower and change in our suite, I instructed the boys to have a pee before heading out for some sight-seeing. Mothers are cunning people. They so often take the fun out of life by instructing you to pee at home which then, because you're now dehydrated, makes you miss out on having a swazz in a strange communal loo. Justyn comes out of the bathroom wiping his mouth with the back of his hand.

"Justyn! I told you not to drink from the taps," I admonished him.

"I didn't, Trisch, I promise." He replied, near to tears as he was so frightened of displeasing anyone, let alone me. He was ten years old and in a city without either of his birth parents, a chick who gave instructions in sharp staccato sentences, and a step-brother who was already in his teenage years and therefore seemed to be a cut above him.

"I found a great water-fountain in the bathroom," he hiccoughed, "I didn't drink from the tap, I swear."

"Whaddaya mean, a water fountain in the bathroom?" This perplexed me for I couldn't remember seeing such a thing when I'd used the shower. "Show me."

So the little guy led me into the bathroom and sombrely, with tears spilling over the bottom of his lids, pointed to the *bidet* and said, "*that* fountain."

Dragging two young kids around Paris to view Montmartre, the Eiffel Tower et al wasn't much fun, especially as they were jet-lagged. I think the drink from the water fountain did not agree with Justyn either as he puked all over the boat we were floating down the Seine on. I ran away and Dane cleaned up.

A couple mornings later, I got the kids into the car and we headed off to Disney. Dane was given the job of official map-reader and navigator. Big mistake. Dane is *rigting bedonnered*. We ended up on a little road heading for some place called Meaux. Every signboard we saw pointed to Meaux, but we never actually got there. I have no idea how far Meaux is from Paris, but we kept heading towards it. Or so the signboards said.

Today I still do not know where Meaux is. Anybody out there know? Where's Meaux? I Think Meaux was more than just a sign because a week later we would meet Mo, our driver in Egypt.

By the time we had spent four days in Euro-Disney, I was Disneyed out. Don't get me wrong, I love Mickey Mouse, but a French

Mickey just doesn't crack it for me. And the queues in the park were so long. It was, after all, summer holidays for the Northern Hemisphere children so Disney life was exceptionally hectic. But that didn't faze us. We would stand in line, waiting patiently to ride the Tea Cups, Coco-pans and Space Mountain, after which Justyn would get autographs from various Disney Characters. Every French kid who could skinnive a couple places further along in the queue would try to do so, pushing my two well-mannered South African boys out of the way. Little poesays. The French kids, I mean.

The adults were just as bad. I'm not saying all French people are poussez, but this was my initiation into their culture and I did not like it one bit. I am sure we just got the bad end of the stick and happened to come across the worst of the nation, but it left an impression that has been hard to change, despite a couple of trips back to France.

It was nearing time for the Cruisin' The Kingdom Parade to start. The boys and I took up our place at a junction off the main road. From there we would have a good view. Kids and adults were lining up along Main Street, jostling for position on the pavements. Before long, I was bumped by a woman who was trying to push her kids in front of us. She wasn't the tallest, but she certainly had bulk and strength in her stocky figure.

"Excuse me!" I exclaimed. You all know that this is a very South African thing to say when you are not quite sure of how a situation is going to pan out.

She gabbled something at me in a language I did not understand and continued to scoot the kids further in front. Now I didn't mind letting the little ones come in front of me at all. What I did mind was that Mama was pushing me completely off balance and my foot was lodged between the street and the concrete pavement edge. My ankle was being crushed.

"Excuse me!" I exclaimed even louder this. "Don't push me!"

They obviously spoke no English and with a final shove from the French Maid, I fell right over onto a burly man who was smoking a nasty smelling cigarette. Well, that did it. He grabbed all 51kgs of me, hoisted me up and plonked me right on top of Dane who himself went down, sending Justyn flying. It was like watching a stack of dominoes go over.

The melee which ensured thereafter was perfect for a black comedy. Everyone who had a voice started shouting, all in weird languages which my brain couldn't compute. Mr Smelly Smoker turned around to me and screamed *'attention!'* in his Gauloises stinky breath, right in my face, spittle splattering across my cheeks. I have no idea what he was screaming for. He had my attention, dammit.

"*Sortir de la voie pour les enfants de s'asseoir,*" he hissed. It sounded a lot more sinister, like 'get out of here or I'll kill you'. But I heard the last bit about arses, and I didn't like it none.

"Attention *jou fokken moer*, you stupid fat, bad smelly French *poussez*! Don't you call me an ass okay? And especially don't you stuff around with a Seouf Efriken chicken and her kids, hey, hey?"

"*Sacre Bleu!*" He responded, flailing his arms around his body, cigarette ash flying in all directions.

I understood that alright, because as I said before, when I'm miffed, as I was that night, I talk twenty different shades of blue.

"*Blerrie bliksem donnerse moer.*"

Hey, I admit. I'm also no hero. I could see I was one *kippie* up against the remnants of the French Foreign Legion. So I backed off, muttering as I herded my kids off to find another spot.

But I did give myself a pat on the back for shouting at them in no uncertain terms, "*julle's maar net 'n klomp poussays!*"

Green-green. Green-green. Pink. Yellow?

Remember tickey boxes?

Those people who were not fortunate enough to have a telephone installed in their homes would stand at the street corner, often for hours, in a queue to use the public pay phones.

Tickey boxes were so called because in 'the old days' one paid a tickey (3d) to make a call. After the 1961 conversion to Rands and cents, tickeys were replaced by a brass 2½ c coin. I still have one in my wallet. Sadly, it's still only worth about 2 ½ cents.

Tickey boxes were not quite like their famous British cousins, but they were painted red. They had the obligatory outward-opening door and a bare light bulb hanging from the centre of the roof which usually did not work. Probably because some schmuck had stolen it.

Call boxes had a particular smell to them which could not be found anywhere else. Opening the door, one's nose would be assailed with the aromas of stale cigarette smoke, infused with the newsprint paper of the directory book which would be hanging on a thick metal chain, dangling downwards, with its pages curling in protest. Acrid urine from hobos and unscrupulous youths were the top note that came through. This was usually why one would, while making a call, stand halfway out the box, with one foot wedged under the door, holding it open. Everyone, naturally, would then be privy to your entire conversation, which is why the neighbourhood always knew what was happening in each other's lives.

My mother, naturally, refused to use a tickey box. She insisted on having a telephone at home. It was situated on the night stand next to her bed and there was always a telephone index book and a 2HB pencil next to it, along with a notepad for taking messages. Coloured olive green, it was the most modern up-to-date telephone which the SA Telephone Services Department could offer. These were called cricket phones, the name derived from the shrill ring made when a call was coming in, reminiscent of a crickets chirping.

Mom also had a lock on the phone. Because she didn't want the maid to use it. I was fascinated when watching my mother make a phone call. It was a ceremony of note. She would sit down on the side of the bed, put her glasses on, rummage in her handbag for a bunch of keys, one of which would fit the back of the cricket phone. Unlocked, Mom would then pick up the pencil, turn it upside down, and put the rubber end into the round slot of the plastic dial. This way, she would dial each number. Then she would pick up a cigarette and light it, and then settle in for a nice long chat.

My aunt and uncle, in contrast, had an archaic phone. It was installed against the wall in the hallway just outside the dining room of their farmhouse. The polished wooden backing board smelt of wax, the dangling black earpiece smelt like my Aunty Gloria's Lux soap.

The shared line was part of an exchange system which was operator driven. But I did not know that then. I would look at it wondrously when my Aunt stood at the phone, talking to the person who lived inside the box. I couldn't understand how all those people she spoke to fitted into that little box.

Many holidays I would spend, hanging around the farmhouse, listening intently to the sequence of rings the phone would make during the day.

One long, three short was the ring for Tannie Jacoba from the farm across the valley.

Two short, one long, one short was the ring I waited for with bated breath.

And when I heard it, I would slip on the polished floor, skedaddelling around the corner to grab the handset and say *"twee nil een, Joubert plaas,* hello?" while standing on tiptoe to see if I could just manage to spy who was inside the box before they answered me.

During the early 1980's, South Africa saw the introduction of the mobile phone.

It first started off with car phones. They were bulky contraptions which slotted into your car and which made you look quite important as you drove down the highway chatting away with a large handset glued to your ear. Of course you made sure to have it against the ear which could be seen through your car window by other drivers stuck in rush hour traffic. As the traffic crawled along, you would smile, gesticulating with the other hand, scrunching up your shoulders so that the other driver would understand what an important call you were on. He would acknowledge your pained expression with a slight nod. And then you'd smirk to yourself because you could almost see the poor guy thinking 'oh my gosh, I wish I could be as important as her and have a car phone in my yellow Volkswagen Beetle.'

Before long, Nokia and Ericsson became household names. These were the only two makes of cell phones available to technology-starved South Africans at the time. You either had a Nokia or you had a brick. I had a brick. My first cell phone was almost half the breadth of the iPad I'm using today to write this memoir, but also about ten times the weight. It was made of a durable black plastic with a small screen which I could barely read anyway, and it had an aerial which needed to be flipped up from the side of the phone in order to receive a signal.

Many business lunches were judged successful by the number of cell phones displayed at each place setting around the table. When one rang, everyone would reach for their phones and pray that it was theirs ringing, almost being disappointed when the screen on their phone didn't light up. The lucky person would flip their aerial, punch at the little green telephone icon and lift the index finger of their other hand in a 'just a moment' sort of gesture. The whole table would go quiet while the fortunate one had his, or in my case, her conversation.

I would give instructions to my secretary to phone me at an appointed time during most lunches just so that my colleagues would know how fortunate I was.

Amazing how technology has changed our lives.

Nowadays we have a vast array of phones which just don't leave us alone. Take my BlackBerry.

Last I looked, Blackberries were the fruit I used to feed my silkworms (ok, smartasses, I know they were mulberries, but in the Orange Free State—see, colour again - they were black, so we called them black berries).

My BlackBerry has become an extension of my right hand. I feel lost without it. I keep my diary on my phone, I talk via

BBM with my kids, I email business contacts on it, hell, I even take photos on the thing. When I'm lost, I use the GPS function to get me back on track and to my destination. When it's dark, I use the screen light to see the keyhole of the door I'm trying to open. I Facebook my mates on it, and they can see where I'm at because my post will show 'posted 3 minutes ago via BlackBerry near Chartwell.'

Occasionally I will be talking on the landline phone set in my office when my cell phone starts to ring. Now the blonde in me comes out and I can never quite work out if I need to ignore the cell phone ringing, dump the landline conversation and answer the BlackBerry, switch the BlackBerry onto silent, or what. What to do?

Sometimes I wish for the simple life. Bring back the old phone. I would so love to pick up the handset, crank the highly-polished brass handle on the side and hear a voice from inside the wooden box say, *"Nommer asseblief?"*

I Guess That's Why
They Call it The Blues
(with apologies to Elton John)

I was a wretched little girl a lot of the time. As the Queen called 2005 her Annus Horribilis, so I called my childhood *Horrendum Kiditous.*

Firstly, my parents were old. I mean they were really old. I was the proverbial surprise baby. I think when my parents realized the bump in my mother's midriff wasn't middle age spread, but rather a baby growing in her womb, they must have had a conniption.

I can just imagine my father's bushy eyebrows raising right up and meeting his receding hairline and exclaiming, "WTF?"

Secondly, they were both sickly. Around my first year of school my mother fell ill. She spent more time in hospital than I can remember her being at home. By the time I turned eleven, she had gone downhill fast. Of course, nobody thought to tell me a thing, after all, in those days children were seen and not heard. And most definitely not given any information which they surely would not understand?

Except that I was nobody's fool. I listened to the adults talking and formed my own opinion on what was happening to my poor mother.

I believe she had cancer. My brother-in-law, years later, told me I was smoking my socks aka talking rubbish. But I know I'm right. I believe my mother had breast cancer. If not, why then did she have purple lines drawn across her chest and why did all the adults talk about radiation in whispered tones while waiting outside the hospital ward at visiting hours?

The day my mother died started off like any other Saturday. My father was standing in the CNA as he did every Saturday morning, flipping through the various magazines before choosing his usual flying journals. It was 11am. I remember this well because Big Ben - the copycat version of the real thing - situated in Welkom, Orange Free State, was chiming 11 o'clock as we came out of the store.

"Daddy, we must go phone Mommy," I said, pulling him by the hand towards the car.

We were visiting with my sister who lived in the thriving mining community of Welkom with her wonderful husband, Peter.

"Yes, yes, yes," my poor father placated me, "we can only phone her later when we get to Alma's house."

My mother had been hospitalised in Pretoria but had been allowed out for the weekend to stay with my cousin Agnes, who was a Registered Nurse.

By the time we got back to my sister Alma's house, had lunch and the obligatory afternoon nap in the warm Free State sun which streamed across the bed I was lying on, I had forgotten the urge to phone my mother.

Television had just been introduced to South Africa and we would sit eagerly waiting for the broadcast to begin, watching the test pattern with the SABC logo and the clock counting down until the station would open with a visual of the South African orange, white and blue flag fluttering in the breeze while some military band or orchestra played the national anthem. And when the anthem played, you were supposed to stand to attention and sing with great gusto and pride.

So it was that Saturday evening in June, the adults were huddled together on the couch in my sister's lounge, while Dee Dee (my niece) and I lay under eiderdowns on the carpet, watching the TV for the start of the evening's entertainment when the phone rang.

It was my Aunty Gloria phoning from the farm. My mother had died. She had keeled over in the loo in Agnes' apartment and had passed away from a massive coronary. At 11am that day.

I remember my sister bursting into hysterical wailing, throwing her body over her husband's wheelchair, kneeling in front of him while he stroked her hair and tried to calm her. No doubt my father was dazed and bewildered. Independent kid that I was, I was torn between the show 'Little House on The Prairie' that was just about to start on TV or join my sister in a wail myself. Wasn't I supposed to be sad? Isn't that how people are supposed to feel when someone dies? Especially if it is their mother? Was there something wrong with me because I didn't feel the need to howl?

To this day, when I hear of a death, I still don't cry. My pragmatic approach kicks in. Build a bridge and deal with it. Organize the funeral, choose the flowers and hymns, pick up the ashes, scatter them... Deal with it.

And then perhaps a cry might just be in order.

I was eight and a half months pregnant when my brother Eric phoned me. It was 25th October 1981.

"I want to scatter Dads ashes," he said over the phone. About time too I thought. They'd been standing on the top of the pelmet in his house for too many years and it creeped me out every time I was asked to draw the curtains there.

"Ok, where and when?" I sighed. I knew my brother. He wasn't going to do this the easy way.

It was a warm day in Welkom. I had moved there to be nearer to my family, leading up to the birth of my illegitimate child. I pulled one of my three summer preggy dresses on and drove up to the airport to meet my brother. He was standing under the wings of the plane, smoking a cigarette and looking like he had a huge hangover. Which he probably did have, seeing as how he spent every night at the M.O.T.H. Club getting slaughtered with other Moths, talking about flying and war years and weeping into their brandies.

I found myself a couple of hours later that Sunday morning strapping my pregnant belly into the right hand seat of the little 2-seater Cessna 150, holding a small cardboard box, wrapped in brown paper and string in my hands. The return address on the parcel was the Crematorium in Bloemfontein.

My father had chosen to be cremated. Or so Eric said. I thought it odd at the time because when my mom had been buried, the plot my father chose was an 'over and under', meaning that mom would be buried 12 feet down with space for dad to rest on top of her when his time came. Typical man, wanting to be on top. But what did I know? My father and Eric had always been very close and at the time of his death I was none the wiser as to what my father's wishes were.

Welkom airport had a control tower, operated solely by Mr Marquard, ATC. He was a grey haired little man, bent over at the waist who walked as if he was constantly tripping on something. The control tower had one hundred and three steps, spiralling upwards around the circular walls. Mr Marquard had a red Addis plastic bucket tied to a rope which he would let down to collect flight plans from the pilots, hauling them (the flight plans that is) up to the top section of the tower where he would log them and then, with a whoosh, he'd let the bucket down again to the pilot waiting patiently at the bottom of the stairs, looking upwards for a sign of the descending red article. If the pilot didn't get out of the way, the bucket might just bonk him on the head and then he'd not be able to fly. In my teenage years, Mr Marquard would occasionally allow me into the top section of the tower where I would watch the radar screen and gaze out over the dusty dry Free State landscape, eagerly looking for aeroplanes on their approach to Welkom airport and desperate to get my hands on the microphones.

That Sunday, Eric had logged a flight plan to who knows where with Mr Marquard. We took off on runway Zero Seven, the wings of the Cessna almost flapping to get airborne. I was only pregnant, not fat.

We flew in silence for about 15 minutes. Eric offered me our late father's Swiss army knife.

"Open it," he instructed, not glancing anywhere near the box lying on my lap. I could see he was going through some sort of emotional melt-down. It's a wonder he hadn't brought a measure of brandy and Coke, mixed into a thermos flask with him to settle his jangling nerves.

Boldly I peeled away the brown tape wrapped around the outer packaging and peered inside at its contents. They weren't as scary as I'd anticipated. The grey ashes in a clear plastic bag look just like the stuff I removed from the fireplace during winter, except they're whiter and grainier. These are the remains of my deceased father. The guy who looked a lot like David Niven, British movie star and novelist. My dad even sported the same moustache, neatly trimmed and cleaned, just a quarter inch above the lip at all times. He kept his hair slicked back with *Brylcreem*, wore silk ascots at his throat and always had a terribly faggoty brown cigarillo dangling between his fingers.

Ripping open the plastic packet, some of the ashes scattered onto my lap. I fluffed them off onto the floor of the plane. Eric's upper body rose and collapsed in a heap. I heard him snort and blubber but I ignored him, concentrating instead on getting the little triangular side window of the cockpit open. As I leaned forward, awkwardly over my very swollen belly and holding the baggie up to the window, instead of the contents being sucked out and blown away with the wind, they blew instead right back in at us.

"Bleh, yeuk, bletch!" I spat and coughed, wiping my mouth with my forearm.

"What's the matter?" Eric hiccoughed through his tears.

"I just got a mouthful of Dad!"

Well, that did it for him. Eric dissolved into a puddle. No longer was he a capable pilot, one who did aerobatics in a little 1600VW-engined bi-winged experimental aircraft, the mercy flight pilot who could land on a barren strip of land, in the dark, in Botswana, amongst a herd of elephants, and not even harm one. He snotted and he cried and he wailed until eventually, I had no option but to take over the controls.

I grabbed the radio microphone and pressed the transmit button.

"Welkom, Welkom, this is Whiskey Mike Foxtrot over," I squawked over the connection, "Mr Marquard, I need your help!"

"Whiskey Mike Foxtrot, are you in distress?" came back an ever-so polite and serene reply.

"Mr Marquard, Eric can't fly the plane anymore."

"Come again Whiskey Mike Foxtrot?"

"He's having a nervous breakdown! Mr Marquard! What do I do?" I shrieked, panic suddenly taking hold of me.

With Mr Marquard's help, I managed to get the plane into an auto-pilot circuit around Welkom airport for half an hour. I tried cajoling my brother to take back control of the plane and land it. I became the parent, he the child. Then I took on the child role, trying to kick the adult side of him back into gear. Thirty long minutes it took until finally, the idiot blew his nose, took the plane off autopilot and brought us down safely.

Now understand this. I am not, nor have I ever wanted to be, a pilot. Oh, both Eric and Alma have been there and done that, but me? I prefer to keep my feet on terra firma and leave the heavens for the angels to play in.

And those angels were having a field day, blowing my father right back in my face and making me fly a plane while my brother pulled out from behind his seat, a 2litre Coke, doctored with a good dose of KWV brandy.

Blue for a Boy, Pink for Another Boy

At twenty years old I didn't realise the implications of falling pregnant, especially considering the man I was sleeping with would never acknowledge to his family that he was going to become a father. He wasn't a bad man, he was just Greek. And Greek boys have Greek mothers. And Greek mothers do not want their Greek sons to marry anyone other than a good Greek girl. Which I was not. Neither Greek nor good.

But our love affair was sweet and kind and gentle and we truly enjoyed being with each other. Except that I was forbidden fruit and so in turn I was hidden from view. The family did not know about me. And that's the way it was kept.

I was on the pill. Well, I was on the pill when I remembered to take it. At nineteen, pill taking was a drag. Even drug type pills. I never did them. My friends were always taking something called 'No-Bees' to get high or down, I'm not sure which. Apparently they were also good tabs for losing weight. Which I did not need. I was quite skinny enough. All knobbly knees, a ribcage you could play the washboard on and no boobs.

I was happily in love even though it was a secret one. Until I fell pregnant. Naturally the first thought my beau had was to 'get rid of it'. I wasn't happy about being pregnant either and initially I did entertain the thought of having an abortion. In the early 1980's abortions were illegal in South Africa so one had two choices. Actually, three. Go to a butcher in the back alleys of Hillbrow and hope to G-d you didn't die from blood loss and being butchered, go over the border to Lesotho where abortion was legal, or have the child. I considered all the options.

The day my Greek god came to fetch me to drive down to Lesotho, I just couldn't do it. I stood on the steps of my apartment block crying while he shouted that his life would be ruined if I didn't go through with it. I realised then he'd just become a god-damned Greek.

I knew that day that something special was about to happen in my life and I just could not go through with an abortion.

I thank Hashem every single day for the beautiful son that I gave birth to in November that year.

I packed my little burgundy coloured VW Lux Bug with all my possessions and headed south to the Free State. My sister had convinced me that I needed to 'come home' to have my baby. She had just lost a little boy at close to full term and was suffering from post-partum depression. Frankly, she was just permanently depressed anyway, but losing her child sent her right over the edge.

For as long as I could remember, Alma had always been manipulative, but in this instance she was unscrupulous and controlling. Along with her husband (the drop-out she'd left Peter for), they tried to persuade me to give my baby up for adoption saying they would take it on as their own. They threw everything in the book at me. From the 'we are a married couple so he'll have a Dad in his life', to 'you can't afford a baby'. But again, this was something I just couldn't do. I could not give the life I had started to feel moving in my belly away, not even to strangers, and especially not to them.

One morning during the last trimester of my pregnancy, there was a knock on my apartment door. I opened it to find two strange women peering in, trying to look past me into my little home. On asking who they were and why they wanted to come in, I was shocked to hear that they were from Child Welfare Services. I invited them in with absolute fear and trepidation.

"Your family are concerned that you will not be able to look after a child." The one woman said to me. "They want us to convince you to give the child up for adoption. We need to assess your living circumstances and finances and make a report."

I was so upset that my own sister could pull such a fast and nasty plot. In fact, until Dane was a couple of months old, I stopped speaking to her and did not see her. I was fed up with how cruel she had become. I had tried to understand her depression and the loss of her own baby, but she had turned vicious and I did not want to be faced with her malice.

Showing the welfare ladies my little flat furnished with all my late father's furniture and some of the baby stuff I had already started buying, I pulled out my bank book. There, in bold letters, was enough money to not only see me through my pregnancy, but also to look after my child after his birth until I could get a job. They were quite satisfied and left me fuming and really rather hormonally angry. About a month before my due date, these two ladies returned with a baby bath filled with goodies for my new child. They had knitted the most beautiful baby jackets and booties. One of these ladies would later become the day mother that I would leave Dane with while I went to work.

Going back to Welkom, where I had spent the last couple

years of my high school life, as an unmarried pregnant woman, was quite interesting to say the least. I was either seriously dumb and naive, or I was thick-skinned. I can't say which even to this day. While at school I had been seen as a prim and proper girl, never likely to be kissed, never mind get pregnant. So it was fabulously scandalous to be expecting and unmarried in those years. I became the source of many a good *skinner* session in the local community as well as a turn-on to dreadful old married men who had nothing better to do than think about having sex with anyone other than their wives. I was accosted many a time by these losers, most of them being drinking buddies of my brother. Say no more.

One of them was a grey-haired skinny horrible nasty looking man who thought that he could buy his way into my bed. I hated him for even thinking I would consider such an awful proposition. It was mostly in the evenings when he and my brother were plastered that he would become lecherous and fall all over me, trying to impress me with his sexual innuendos and offerings of becoming a kept woman. I would flee their company and hide out with my sister-in-law and the children in the main bedroom of her house.

A couple of days before my due date I was sitting in Dr Bonet's rooms. He was a lovely gentle elderly general practitioner who was looking after me. I did not go to a gynaecologist or obstetrician for my internment. In those days, GPs could even perform minor operations like appendectomies and so on.

Dr Bonet was instructing me about taking a dose of liquid paraffin if the baby did not make its appearance by the 4th of November. Of course, I did not listen properly and so, on due date, I sat in my sister-in-laws kitchen, slugged a bottle of liquid paraffin and then proceeded to eat an orange which I subsequently threw up. I still, to this day, do not eat oranges. Patensie or not. Which reminds me, Carel was right, those Patensie oranges, were the sweetest of sweet. Before they went *vrot*, Peter made them into Patensie Marmajam... they were just too sweet to be classed as marmalade, and just too tart to be called jam.

My first beautiful boy came into the world easily and with great speed that night. He hasn't stopped being in a hurry since his birth 31 years ago.

Around 11pm I woke up with what I thought was a tummy ache. My belly was as hard as a football. And just as round. The ache eased somewhat and I dozed off again. A while later, I woke with the same sensation and lay awhile wondering if this was the time or not.

I had watched a movie of giving birth at the local clinic a month before so I was a bit confused as my waters had not broken. I picked up the telephone and called my sister-in-law, interrupting her bridge game.

"Ash, I think I'm in labour, my tummy keeps going hard."

"How far apart?" she asked, thinking of the last finesse she had just, well, er, finessed.

"I don't know... maybe two or three minutes?" I don't have a watch handy. It's late at night, it's dark, I'm sitting on the loo because I'm convinced my bowels need to work. Which they aren't obliging me with.

"Get yourself to the hospital right away," she exclaims, "I'll be there as soon as I've finished my game."

Alright, alright, that was just a little bit of artistic author-type what's-it-called when you make it sound more exciting stuff? She wasn't really so callous as to finish her game first. She is the most wonderful woman and on the night of 4th November, Ashné (knowing her) probably put her cards down gently, conceded to the other team and said "I have to go" without an explanation.

Once in the ward at the government hospital, the midwife,

after examining me, turned to my sister-in-law and said "go home, my dear, this is going to be a long night and the baby will probably only come tomorrow sometime. We'll phone you when she's due to deliver."

This was around 1.30am. That time of night when everything is so quiet you hear noises when there aren't really any to hear. It's just the noise of the night. So I kept quiet myself. I really didn't want to add to the plinks and ta-dums and aaaah's coming down the maternity ward corridors. So I kept quiet and eventually fell asleep again.

I'm not going into the gruesome bits of delivery here—I can just see Dane's face as he reads this, suffice it to say the next morning I waddled off to the phone booth in the maternity ward's lounge and phoned my friend Linda in Durban.

"My little boy was born at 2.25am this morning." I told her proudly.

We went through the normal questions following the birth of a baby. Weight? Length? Apgar? Name? Dane Eric.

"What did it feel like giving birth?" she shouted eagerly down the trunk call phone line, wanting to hear all the gory news.

"Lou, it was just like having a big shit."

And so, five and a half years later, this time, lying in a private clinic, with a gynaecologist on hand, a husband at my side, and a Granny looking after Dane, I looked forward to delivering my second child.

I had just started a new job when one of my colleagues mentioned she thought I was getting a bit fat around the middle. I looked at her in astonishment when she suggested I might be pregnant.

Me? Pregnant? Don't be crazy. I was married to a barn owl

who stayed up all night in his workshop tinkering around on old tractors and cars while I watched TV and went to bed alone. We hardly had sex, how could I get pregnant?

As sure as G-d made little boys, I had one growing inside of me.

The first person I told once I'd left Dr Kikko's rooms was my friend Jane. I went around to her apartment and sat staring into my coffee cup. How was I going to tell my husband I was pregnant? We had just purchased a large piece of land and built a small house for us and an en-suite cottage for his mother. He was without a secure job and I had just started a new one. I was petrified of going home with the news.

But, as he opened the gate for me I took the bull by the horns and shouted through the open window of the little green Renault 4, "I have a bun in the oven!" His face turned red and then the biggest smile I had ever seen before (and never seen since) spread across his face and he almost whoop-whooped right there.

Barn Owl became Daddy Pigeon. He strutted around with his chest puffed out, telling everyone he was going to become a Dad. It was one of the few moments in our life together when I saw him excited.

My pregnancy was easy. I did the usual gynae checks, each time asking if we could tell the sex of the baby. I wanted to be prepared. We didn't really have the money to decorate a baby room, but if we did, I'd like it to be the right colour.

"I'm 99.9% sure it's a girl," Dr Kikko said, looking at the monitor of the 2-D scan he was doing. No 3-D let alone 4-D scans like they have nowadays back then.

I sat thinking of pretty girls names and finally decided on Jade Christie which would honour my mother-in-law's name, having the same initials as hers. She was tickled pink (pardon the pun) when she heard the news.

Talking pink, I started knitting a little pink and white matinee jacket. Considering I was not by any means a knitter, I was rather proud of the finished item, despite the few mistakes on it. I mean, what is a slipped stitch here or there?

One day at the office, just prior to going on maternity leave, everyone disappeared early for lunch. We had a great canteen which served fabulous lunches and I made good use of it each day. Especially while I was eating for two. My stomach growled and I suddenly realised I'd been left behind that day. Often I walked up to the canteen with one of my colleagues, but looking around that day, I noticed all the desks were vacated.

Quite miffed about their lack of concern for a pregnant fairy, I muttered as I climbed the stairs to the first floor canteen.

"Surprise!" they all shouted as I walked in. There were pink ribbons and streamers hanging from the ceiling with a banner attached to the wall announcing 'It's a GIRL!' in pink with glittery silver edging. Napkins in pink with white polka dots and a delicious looking strawberry mousse cake in the centre of the table made my tummy growl even more. 'Good Luck and Welcome Baby Jade!' was iced in white curly sugar work on the cake.

Every gift I received that day was in beautiful shades of pink with white accents for the little girl who I was supposed to deliver in 4 weeks. I went on maternity leave that following Friday with thoughts of a blue eyed pretty girl wearing cute dresses and pink bobbles in her long blonde hair.

Wake up call. Monday morning should have been a Friday because it was the 13th of July. Trundling along at a snails' pace (thank goodness my little car couldn't go faster) with Dane in the passenger seat, a very fancy silver BMW shot out from a stop street at left and smashed into the side of my little French piece of crap.

I got out of the car, gathered my son into my arms and walked to the side of the road while the women driver of the BMW was screaming obscenities at me for not stopping in time.

"You idiot!" I shouted back once I had caught my breath, "you were the one who jumped a stop street!"

I put Dane down on the pavement next to me and gathered my maternity dress up to wipe the blood from his knee. An ambulance arrived and before I knew it I was on my way to the gynae's rooms for an emergency scan to check that my unborn baby had not been hurt in the accident.

"Um," Dr Kikko scratched his chin, "you know that point zero one percent chance your baby isn't a girl? It's not a girl."

"Whaaaat? But I've got pink stuff for her."

"Him."

"Him? Not her? You sure not her? Him?"

"100% sure." He answered glumly.

Now I was stuffed. I had loads of girly things at home. Hell, I had a girly name. I'd even knitted in pink for gawd's sake.

For two weeks, I ran around various stores, begging to exchange some of the gifts I'd received from pink to white. I wasn't taking any chances that perhaps that point zero one percent was ninety-nine point nine percent wrong. Fortunately most store managers were accommodating, but there were many, many items I was unable to change.

On due date, I took my suitcase with me to my appointment with Dr Kikko. As I explained to him, if Dane had been a quick one, this baby was surely not going to hang around either once he/she/it was ready to make his/her/its appearance. I was not taking any chances and best he induce me there and then. I was not going home. *Finish en klaar.*

Dr Kikko did not disagree. I think he saw that arguing with

me was quite pointless, and so I found myself booking into the maternity section of the private clinic a few minutes later.

Lying back in the bed in a darkened room, with an IV going into me to induce labour, I was quietly enjoying the last moments of being pregnant when a little man carrying a bunch of tubing whooshed in like an apparition and said he was there to do a spinal block.

"A spinal what?" I asked, baffled. "Who ordered it?"

"Your Doctor did."

"I don't want one."

"Why?"

"Coz I don't. No-one's putting a needle in my back." I folded my arms over my belly and puffed my cheeks.

"Are you sure?" he quizzed, adding, "It's nice. It's really not sore and you'll feel so much better afterwards."

"You ever had one?" I returned.

"No..." he trailed off as he saw my one finger pointing towards the door.

"Well, if you haven't had one, how can you say it's nice? Bugger off! I don't want one!"

He disappeared in a huff and slammed the door behind him. I figure he muttered all the way down the passage about losing out on a hefty fee.

"I want to push!" I huffed at the orderly pushing me into the operating theatre.

"No! Not yet!" He cried. I could see in his eyes he was a newbie on the block and had never been faced with a woman panting the way I was.

"Nurse! Nurse!" He looked around for someone to help him. There was an expression of panic on his face and a wild look in his eyes.

"I want to push!" I reiterated. This time with just a smidgeon of intensity and a decibel or two louder than the last time.

A facecloth was shoved into my face and a voice sounding like it belonged to a drill sergeant instructed me to do nothing of the sort, to breathe through it, and to wait until the Doctor came through from prepping himself.

Now, you know me. Tell me not to do something, I do it. And so, at 8.20pm on the night of July 22, 1987, I delivered my beautiful son, Wade William, weighing in at 2.52kg and 50cm long with a normal Apgar right there in the corridor of the theatre complex.

Then I got up, dressed him in a beautiful pink onesie with pink socks and a pink bonnet and I took him home.

Foo Blue Stinky Poo

We had just moved into our villa in Egypt when I had my first experience with a FICCS—a very derogatory acronym I made up for the Egyptians—Flea Infested Camel... you've worked out the rest I'm sure.

I walked up a very uneven pathway. It looked like a copy of the Nubian sandstone path at Luxor temple. From the gate to the front door was probably twenty paces. Fortunately I had flat sandals on so my ankles didn't break, even though it felt like they would.

I entered the French-style villa in Maadi, Cairo and looked around with great trepidation. Stepping over the threshold into a large, double volumed entrance hall, I was faced with the most awful looking wooden staircase with an even worse wooden handrail.

The first time I viewed the villa which Peter had already signed the contract on, I was sure my husband had lost his marbles. In addition to the staircase, the so-called TV lounge had no floor. It was a sandpit. Any kindergarten group would have had great fun there. All they needed was buckets and spades. I kid you not. It was a huge room filled with sand and surrounded by four walls which were not yet painted. There was Arabic graffiti sprayed on the walls in green lacquer. I was later told it was a prayer for the workers to work well.

"Are you crazy!" I picked my way over old Siwa water bottles and foul smelling Cleopatra cigarette butts in the sand back to the entrance hall.

"I can't see myself ever sitting in this room watching Wheel of Fortune."

I gave Peter one of those you-stupid-idiot-why'd-you-choose-this-dump kinda looks. He was standing there already defending his decision with placating gestures while Mohammed our driver paced nervously behind him. The kids had already disappeared "*fohk*" to check out their bedrooms.

Engineer Salah stuck his head around the door jamb.

"Meesta Beeda, Madame N'Rish," he couldn't say Trisch, "You 'appy? En'sha'allah."

I learnt quickly that all Egyptians use the phrase *en'sha'allah* (G-d willing) in every other sentence and with fervent belief that if Allah really wills it, then it will happen. What worried me is that they often did nothing themselves, waiting for Allah to will it. And then you could wait for bloody ages because most times they were incredibly lazy and didn't get off their butts to at least try and start getting Allah to will it.

"You can choose brand new tiles to put on the floor," Peter encouraged me. He could see the look on my face. When my nose pulls up in disgust and the edges of my lips go white, he knows I'm not a happy camper. Usually he walks away and leaves me to calm down, but this time he knew he had some serious spade work to do to placate me.

"You can also choose the paint colour you want on the walls," he added. Engineer Salah pulled the arm of a workman and instructed him to show me the different colours I could choose from. If you think they produced little square pieces of paper in different hues and shades, sorry for you, no cigar.

Instead, the worker brought a bucket of white paint into the room, dipped his forefinger into a bottle of red dye, dripped a couple of drops into the white paint and boom-ba-la-boom we had pink paint. He then painted a large square on the wall and grinned at me, nodding his head and saying, *"Tamem, Madame, tamem?"* (Ok, Madam, ok?)

You know, I had to laugh. If I hadn't, I would have cried. And that would have made my mascara run. All in all, the revamping of the villa went along at great speed and before we knew it, our furniture had arrived from South Africa.

But not before we had sheep bleating in our basement and then bloody handprints stamped all over the walls. I kid, er, lamb, you not.

The white walls of the basement were dirtied with bloody hand prints along with Arabic writing of the name Allah interspersed here and there, also in dripping blood. This comes from an Islamic tradition of sacrificing an animal on the holiday of Eid Al-Adha and then smearing the blood around the premises of a new business, a home, or on the outer paintwork of a car for good luck. There was no good luck for me when I saw the sheep poo on the ceramic tiles—especially when I worked out I didn't yet have a maid and would have to clean it up myself.

I put my foot down flat when they wanted me to partake of the slaughtered lamb. I know I sound like a city slicker. I am one. Yes, I know where our meat comes from. But I just didn't want that poor sheep's last glance from its stricken eyes to be focused on me. And then be eaten by me too. No way Jose. Thank you very much. Goodbye.

There was great jubilation the night our container was brought in from Alexandria. Even the kids helped unpack the four hundred and twenty eight boxes, excluding the wooden casks holding TVs and the antique upright Spathe piano. Dane dusted it down, then sat down and started playing. To our amazement, it was still in tune. And believe you me, both of us are pitch perfect so we'd have soon got tuning it if it wasn't. Justyn had the *scale electrix* out on his bedroom floor, clothes and books, toys and shoes lying scattered around and completely forgotten in his excitement of having his 'stuff' again. Peter was checking box numbers off against his list and I was shouting '*henna*' pointing fingers to various rooms of the entrance hall and '*fok*' which not only meant upstairs you dirty sons of bitches, but also '*fok*, I didn't realize we had so much shit.'

The villa, as I mentioned before, had an awful staircase. I stood in the entrance hall one day, looking up and wondering what I could do about the eyesore before me. Short of telling Peter to rip it out and build a new one, I had to come up with a fabulous idea. Images from Garden and Home went through my head.

"Eureka!" I shouted. Both kitties who'd been weaving around my ankles suddenly went all witch like, arched their backs, gave a huge hiss and disappeared upstairs, one into Peter's underwear shelf and the other under the comforter on our bed. They were creatures of habit.

I grabbed my purse, went out to the road and got a taxi down to Omar Effendi, the local government store.

One week later, the carpet guy arrived to lay a carpet up the staircase and affix brass rods at each step. *Tré impressive*, I think. Great way to hide those awful wooden stairs too.

Round one. I leave the carpet man, who speaks no English, under the watchful eye of Calistos our Nigerian houseman, to install the carpet and rods. Happily, I disappear off to have breakfast with a South African friend on Road 9.

Breakfast at Lucille's consists of a stack of American pancakes, maple syrup, golden brown fried bananas and Macon. No pork served in Egypt (unless you know the Swiss Butcher). Huge cups of weak coffee downed during breakfast with the ladies makes me need to pee, so off I rush off to the loo. Just as I flush it, the entire building starts to tremble and I nearly wet myself all over again. My heart beats in triple time, my mouth goes dry and I can't get the rickety door of the bathroom open fast enough. I'm relieved to find out it is not an earthquake such as they had in the 1980s but just the local metro train rattling past on its way to Tahrir Square, which, by the way, is not a square, it's a large circle outside the Cairo Museum.

Belly full from my breakfast, I amble happily back into the villa. A beautiful carpet with shiny brass poles cascading down the staircase appeases my *magies vol, oogies toe* vision. But something is just not right and I can't quite work it out. Not only do I have an amazing sense of smell, but I can also tell if a picture is just a half a degree off alignment on the wall. And there's something squiffy about this scene.

I tentatively approach the staircase. One step up, all's ok. Another step up, looks alright again. Ten steps up and I get to the corner. Got it. The carpet angles at the corners were non-existent. One piece was purely laid over the other, sort of like a plait one would make in your apple pie pastry.

In pigeon Arabic and with a lot of hand movement and finger pointing, the carpet man finally understands I'm not happy with the workmanship. He needs to remove it and take it back to Omar Effendi and get it done properly with angles at the corners. *Doulwati*! Now!

Round Two. Peter's secretary Maha informs me that they will bring back the carpet fixed and angled and stitched neatly in place. Again, I leave Calistos to handle the FICCS who have kicked their shoes off at the door and are padding in their smelly holey socks over my new Persian carpet in the entrance hall towards the offending wooden staircase.

This time, however, I do not go to Lucille's. I stay in the TV lounge—which now sports beautiful white tiles on the floor and a subtle shade of white with just a *tikkie* blue paint on the walls. Calistos comes into the lounge a while later, looking almost as pale as the walls I had just been hanging pictures on.

"Madame, they say they are finished." He almost bows at me. I really can't get used to this subservient mannerism he insists on displaying.

"Oh for fucks sake, Calistos, get up!" I shout at him, irritated at his prostrations.

I get off the step-ladder, Calistos starts stammering, but I sweep past him, up the two steps to the entrance hall and stop dead in my tracks. In front of me is a lovely blue carpet, going up the staircase, bright shiny brass poles secured at each step. Again I figure something is cock-eyed here but what? I take a step closer, then another, then I get it. The blue carpet is edge-stitched with white cotton thread.

You know when you slap yourself on your forehead and you give yourself such a miserable headache you just want to vomit? That's what happened to me but I think it was more from the smelly socks than from anything else.

But, having decided I needed to be more accepting of the middle-eastern way of doing things, I try to explain that he must take the carpet away and redo the white edging with blue. He has a doff look on his face. He does not understand.

Calistos tries to explain in his own take on Arabic, but he too gets the same blank expression staring straight back at him.

I have another one of my famous visions and I rush into Dane's room, grabbing a blue koki pen from off his desk. I call the carpet layer man up to the top of the staircase and motion for him to get down on all fours. I do the same.

"This," I take the koki and start colouring in the white thread, "this must be same-same, *fehemt*?" I motion and point and colour some more, asking all the while if he understands. Same same. Point at edging, point at carpet body. Same same, point at white thread, colour it blue. Same same. This is the universal meaning in Egyptian slang for this must be the same as that. Same same. The thread must match the blue of the carpet. I see the hamster spinning in the wheel in his eyes. He stands up proudly and exclaims *'aiwa!'* yes! *'ana fehemt'* I understand. Then I think the hamster fucked off too.

Happy in the knowledge that my kitchen Arabic is easily understandable, I go back to the TV lounge and continue with my chores, ignoring the sounds of the carpet man moving up and down the squeaky staircase.

"Madame," Calistos appears once again, bowing and scraping as he is adamant on doing. "The man must come back tomorrow. He is not finished."

"What do you mean, not finished, Calistos? Not finished what?"

He beckons for me to follow him.

I round the first corner of the staircase and once again get that nasty stinky foot smell. It's enough to put me off gorgonzola for life. This time, however, there's another pong, much stronger than the Stilton hum wafting around the bannister. I recognize it, but I can't quite place it.

Then I see the carpet man, holey stockinged heels, toes digging into the third stair from the top, bum in the air, colouring in the white cotton thread of the fabulously blue carpet with a Yoken indigo-blue permanent marker.

You wanted same same, Madame? You got it. Same same.

RED, WHITE 'N BLUE, WHO THE FUCK ARE YOU?

Many Americans, in my opinion, are seriously under-travelled... if there's such a word? If it isn't, you understand what I mean, don't you?

Oh, they might have gone into space, landed a billion dollar bug called Curiosity on Mars and invented the Internet 28 years ago, but baby, they don't know their Kenya from their Kazakhstan.

Take this. I meet a guy who lives in New York State in Dane's local pub called The Flipside. Peter and I were visiting Dane in Rochester, NY, one April. Friday nights Dane fried fish at The Flipside. Living in a largely Catholic community, fish was on the menu at the pub on Fridays. As Dane says, he got dinner and a drink while on the job, and the fifty bucks they paid him was enough to pay for beer when he went out with his mates later in the evening.

We met I-Yam at The Flipside. He was a rather large and rounded man with a haircut the Army would have been proud of. His shirt was crisp and he wore a string-tie at his throat.

His I 'heart' NY Yankees cap was pulled down over his eyes, possibly to shade them from the spotlight he found himself in when at The Flipside on Fridays. He slurped his beers, sitting at the corner of the bar and occasionally he would lean over to grab the microphone from Slinky the barmaid. And then he would sing. I-Yam thoroughly enjoyed the karaoke sessions held at The Flipside on Fridays.

We nick-named him I-Yam because he sang Neil Diamond's hit "I Am, I Said" off-key with each word running into the other. To this day, when the great Jazz Singer's hit is played on the radio, Peter and I burst out into our very best rendition of "I YAM, I said".

So, sitting at the end of the pub, I-Yam enquires where we come from.

"Johannesburg, South Africa." I politely reply.

Normally I would answer 'Jo'burg', but in America you not only answer in full, but you also have to explain which state you're referring to. This is because the country is so huge they must have run out of town names as they discovered and settled across the continent as so many are duplicated and even triplicated. So if I'd just left my answer at 'Johannesburg' he might have thought I meant Johannesburg, Wisconsin. Which I did not know existed until I Googled it.

"I met a guy once who came from Nairobi," I-Yam says to me, "do you know him? His name is..."

Fill in the blank yourself. Pick a name, any name. Go on... chances are someone reading this book will know that person, don't you think? Now that we have (thanks to the Americans, you gotta love 'em) the internet, email, Twitter and Facebook, the six degrees of separation, I'm sure, are way down to five, or maybe even four. So probabilities of me knowing that person in Nairobi, despite the fact I've only ever been there once in my life, might well be plausible.

Likewise, I was in a hotel in Kissimmee, Florida one year and the darling waitress who must have been in her fifties at the time gets chatting.

"You're from South Africa?" she exclaims wide eyed in a delightful Southern drawl.

"Uhum," I nod, my mouth filled with bacon and eggs.

"And y'all speak English?" She exclaims with even greater awe.

"Uhum," I nod again thinking, yeah ain't that the language we're conversing in?

"And you're white!"

Well, no lady, I'm actually under pigmented and I've not done a spray tan in a while. What the hell. The devil on my right hand shoulder tugged at my ear again, as it is want to do, and whispered… Go on, tell her you live in a mud hut and go to work on the back of an elephant.

Two of our children were indeed very fortunate to be educated at an American International School. Dane graduated from Cairo American College. Their graduation ceremony was held at the foot of the Sphinx. How awesome is that. He then went on to study at Berklee College of Music in Boston, MA. While living there, he met and fell in love with a young man named Ben. They moved in together and before long, the two love birds settled in Upstate New York to be near Ben's family, who also fell in love with Dane.

Not being a student any longer, we cut off Dane's allowance. Suddenly he had to find work. While Ben had a good job, bringing in good money, Dane needed to contribute to their home life as well and so he took a job with the local Catholic Church as their organist.

Dane loved it and he thrived well in the community, until things went sour in his personal relationship. He moved into the dinkiest little house, licking his wounds and trying to move on with his life. Little did we know, but at that stage, Dane's visa expired and he didn't even realise it. After all, there was no expiry date written on the visa. It had been issued in Egypt. Say no more.

Fast forward ten years.

Peter and I are eagerly waiting at the airport to welcome Dane home. It is the first time he has been back in six years and he is filled with trepidation. He had been seeing a lawyer in the USA to try and sort out his visa requirements. They finally went to court and the ruling was that he had to come back to his home country to apply for a work visa.

I am shocked at the sight of the gaunt young man with long red hair who comes through the automatic doors. This surely cannot be the vibrant young man we know as our son? He is thin and clearly stressed. There are dark circles under his eyes and I know that's not from jet lag.

As all mother's do, I mother my son. I feed him, trying to get some fat back on his bones. Peter and I council him as best we can, trying to help him. He finally gets an appointment to see the Consulate to apply for his work visa.

Suffice it to say, he didn't get it and this made me wonder all over again whether or not racism had something to do with it.

Here was this young white male being interviewed by a bulky black dude from Louisiana who clearly did not believe that a white boy, who had been brought up by a mother who embraced Judaism, who had been schooled in a middle eastern country and had an offer to work in a Catholic Church was not a terrorist.

Of course he didn't believe it. And so he stamped 'denied' all over Dane's documentation. This young man had embraced the country, he was working hard, he was paying taxes. He just didn't have the right visa which he was trying to put right.

He hung your red, white and blue flag proudly outside his door.

So I ask the Americans, why is it ok to bring people like the 'lost boys' to your country, to be adopted by white people, given citizenship and who can now run in the Olympics as Americans? Why is it ok to turn a blind eye to Mexican people who have crawled across your borders and are living in your country illegally? And you don't arrest them when they march down your streets during strikes?

When all this young man wanted was to live and work in a country he loved... legally.

LILAC AND LOVE FOR MY YIDDISHE MAMMA

*A*shné was my Yiddishe Mamma. She had met my brother when he played in a band in the early seventies in Bloemfontein. She co-owned a hair-dressing salon in the hotel that the band played in and no doubt my brother, who in those days was quite a handsome bugger, went down for a cut and ended up charming the pants off her.

Ashné was a widow with two young children. She was a beauty too, with auburn hair that shone with health and almond shaped eyes fringed with dark lashes, inherited from her Ashkanazi ancestors. Most importantly, she had an inheritance which my brother would destroy in the blink of an eye.

They married in court and had a hum-dinger of a party that night. Ashné's parents and my parents were both shocked. Neither set were happy about their offspring marrying out of their faiths. Yet both put on a happy show and supported their children. But behind their backs all hell let loose about the bloody goy and the Jewess who'd defied them all and fallen in love.

Within a year or so, Ashné delivered Errol, a beautiful and

intelligent child, whose life would be cut short just as he was reaching adulthood. Two years after his birth, Natalie would make her entrance into the world with a mop of bright red hair and a blood mismatch which would result in her being rushed to Cape Town for a full blood transfusion when she was but hours old. Little tyke, she not only survived but is one of the feistiest and most beautiful women today, still with her red hair and a skin so ivory it would do any soap advert justice.

Eric spent the better part of his marriage to Ashné drunk. He moved their family around, promising them that the next job would be the one, that the next move would be the last. He only held down jobs for a while, his drunken binges putting an end to his employment. Suffering from delusions of grandeur, he squandered every last cent of Ashné's inheritance, plunging their family into debt and bringing them close to the bread-line.

Yet this amazing woman stuck with her husband, working herself to a standstill to support him, all the while teaching her children (and me) the values of her faith, despite my brother's growing anti-semitic views.

When asked by her best friend, Charlene, if she ever regretted marrying Eric, she simply replied, "How could I? Look at the wonderful children he gave me."

Ashné bought me my first pair of jeans from the outfitters store her father owned. The jeans were lilac and I chose a blue and white striped tank top and navy blue clogs to go with them. I wore those jeans until they could not fit me anymore.

Ashné taught me to bake and to cook. She taught me to love and to laugh. I learnt, through her gentle caring and compassionate nature, that being humble was a characteristic I admired. She showed me that while she herself had so little, she was generous with what she did have.

Ashné taught me to say the prayers over the candles on shabbas.

וְיָתוֹ צֵמֶב וְנֵשְׁדְּק רְ שָׁא סֵלֹוֵעָ הֵלֵמ וְנֵיֵהֵלֵ אֵ יֵ נֵדָא הֵ תֵא דֵוֹרֵ ב
שֵדוּק תֵיֵבֵשׁ לֵשׁ רֵנ קֵילֵדֵהֵל וְנֵרֵצֵו

Baruch a-ta A-do-nay Elo-hei-nu me-lech ha-o-lam a-sher
ki-dee-sha-nu bi-mitz-vo-tav vi-tzi-va-noo li-had-leek ner shel
Sha-bbat ko-desh.

Blessed are you, Lord our G-d, King of the universe, who has
sanctified us with His commandments, and commanded us to
kindle the light of the Holy Shabbat.

Every Friday night, I remember my wonderful sister-in-law
as I bring the spirit of Shabbat into our home.

BLACK AND WHITE, LOVE AND LIGHT

I have an adopted sister. She wasn't really adopted in the eyes of the law. She also wasn't adopted by my parents. She was adopted by me.

It's not only because she married Pete van Hees, who has always been, and always will be, my brother-in-law come father come protector come advisor etcetera etcetera. It's also because if I ever wanted a sister to be like a sister, Mandy fitted the bill just perfectly.

I first met her up at the stables. She was a slight young thing with short fair hair sitting atop a very imposing gelding which was snorting and stomping and swishing his head backward and forward. You would have thought removing his nuts would have calmed his temper.

"Stop your nonsense, Brutus," she yelled at him. The horse backed up and settled down. He clearly understood who was in the driving seat.

As well as working on the mines in the drafting office, Mandy was a Farrier. She shod horses which were mostly ten times bigger and heavier than her. But she'd get the horse settled and with precise and quick work, it would soon have a new set of shoes in no time. She rode dressage and also jumped, winning many ribbons at equestrian events throughout the country.

Mandy and Pete married quietly and decided to buy a small farm in the Lejweleputwa District which is mostly an agricultural area, near Welkom. They built a set of stables on their property. Mandy would take in horses for training, working them in the cold Free State mornings before the ice had melted on the duck pond. On one such cold morning, Mandy was working a beautiful horse, when he unexpectedly threw her.

"I knew my back was broken," she says, "the minute I hit the ground."

Now there were two in wheelchairs.

How I admire this astonishing couple. Despite their disabilities, they continued to live on the farm, now going on for nearly three decades. It's not a large farm, but considering they only have two farmhands and one housemaid, it must be a huge undertaking to keep it going. Especially when they're both confined to wheelchairs.

They are humble folk, without airs and graces.

"You have to sit on a dining room chair," Mandy says quite pragmatically, "we don't have a lounge suite. If we had one, the only ones to use it would be the dogs."

They have a herd of sheep which produce many Sunday roasts for me. Their Dexter's bring wonderful fresh milk, butter and cream to the table. Occasionally Pete stockpiles the cream, making it into vanilla ice-cream; he also makes fabulous feta cheese. Their breakfast bacon and ham comes straight from the back yard, as do the large free-range eggs. And when Pete sees an animal looking like it's not worth its keep, he knocks it off, hangs it, cuts it up and packs it into the deep freeze.

Mandy started a vegetable garden which yields fresh, organic produce. From rich green spinach and brown onions, to orange carrots, deep red tomatoes and sunny yellow corn; what she plants, she sows. What she sows, they eat. And what they have too much of, she shares generously with folk around town. Many a trip home from visiting them has boxes of produce on the back seat and cooler boxes of meat in the trunk. Her horseradish is one of my Peter's favourite accompaniments to a rare beef roast. Actually, pleb that he is, he even eats it with roasted lamb, foregoing the mint sauce, its source from the plant which grows under the dripping tap outside.

As they both once said to me, "If we could grow coffee beans, tea and sugar cane, we'd have no need to go to the local supermarket!"

Mandy is also an accomplished quilter. Like so many, she has a stash of fabrics which she turns into beautiful patchwork quilt tops on the twenty-one year old Bernina sewing machine which she inherited from her mother. You and I, fit people, would use our foot to control the speed. Mandy can't. So she puts the foot pedal up next to the machine and, with one hand guiding the fabric and the other controlling the speed of the machine, she quilts the tops with the sheep's wool which she's kept from the shearing season and which she's spent hours carefully combing out and packing into a natural batting.

She is also an avid supporter of Border Collie Rescue in South Africa and helps them by fostering dogs which have been rescued and are in the process of finding their 'forever home'. She hops into Peters converted car and drives through to collect dogs which have been abused (and there are far too many for her liking). Then she loves them back to life and finally delivers them to their new families.

Amongst all of this, Mandy has ten border collies of her own. Plus a couple of mutts.

Each afternoon at five o'clock, she opens the kitchen door. In a flurry of black and white fur, yelping and jostling to get into position, Fly, Meg, Beano, Ben, Sam, Kelly, Bones, Frosty, Holly, Scampy, Cheeky and Chaos are taken for a run up in the fields at the back of the farmhouse. And if Johannes, the farmhand, happens to be bringing the sheep in a little late, the girls and boys herd them into their pens before taking off into the brown fields where they run and yelp and jostle each other for their mother's love.

⁓

"Let's go visit Pete and Mandy on Saturday, shall we?" I've just shouted to Peter.

"Sure!" comes back the response, "don't forget to put out the batteries Pete wanted and the blue cotton you bought for Mandy. What wine should I put in?"

I can't wait to see my sister!

KAMEEL KAK IS THE NEW KHAKI

I often wonder if I started writing my Sunday morning emails to document our adventure in Egypt, or to keep myself sane. It so happens that I have a couple of lever arch files in my office with copies of each email I sent to friends and family, one a week, every week for the 5 years we lived in Cairo. That's a helluva lot of wordage.

It started off with the subject line of that first email reading *Jirre Maar dis Warm Hier in die Kameel Kak.* Jeez, it's hot here in the camel shit.

By week three, my emails were being referred to as *Die Kameel Kak.* By month three, if I missed sending out an email on a Sunday morning, I'd get requests on email from people I didn't even know telling me they'd missed that Sunday's episode and would I please resend to them.

Each Sunday morning, as the boys and Peter headed off to school and work, I would make myself two slices of Marmite toast—no we didn't get Marmite in Egypt, I had packed 24 bottles into our furniture container—I'd pour a nice cup of coffee with two spoons of sugar and a good dollop of long-life milk and then I'd head upstairs to my office. By the time I'd switched on the computer (an XT *nogal!*) had gone through its integrity check and hooked up to the 54K modem which went ka-ping, ka-ping, ka-boing boing boing, as it was connecting, I'd have finished off my breakfast and was ready to get *Kameel Kakking.*

Doffie Sobel, bless her, was a little Yiddishe Bobba. She was four foot nothing, with a white streak in her fringe and a personality bigger than the British isles… not that they have much in the way of personality anyway. Doffie was the widow of Dave Sobel, Mr Pepsi who had also introduced the first canned fizzy drinks, called Groovy, to South Africa. My favourite flavour was the cream soda.

Peter and I were often invited to have Doffies gefilte fish and chopped liver, which she claimed was the best this side of the Dead Sea, but we were only allowed to have it on a Monday night as Peter wasn't allowed at her shabbas table for he was not one of the tribe. This tickled me pink because Doffie wasn't being malicious at all. It was just that she did not have anyone of any other faith at her home on a Friday night. Simple as that. And we loved her for it, and even more, we loved her gefilte fish and chopped liver which we would savour on a Monday night at Dave and Doffie's home. We would pull into the driveway and Uncle Dave would show us to his parking lot which had genuine working parking meters, taking 5c for an hour. We would insert a 20c piece, turn the handle and we knew by 11pm we had better be in that car and on our way before the meter expired.

Peter and Uncle Dave were big Coca-Cola mates. His sudden death hit Peter very hard and he was so touched when, at a very sombre Jewish burial on a grey day in September, Peter was asked to help carry Dave's casket to its resting place. We kept in touch with Doffie over email and always made an effort to visit her when we came back to South Africa on holidays.

About a month after Doffie's death, I received an email from a friend of hers mentioning that Doffie had belonged to a book club. Each month, she would arrive at whoever was hosting the book club meeting that month with the obligatory cake (in Doffies case, probably a kosher one from Shula's Bakery) and the last few weeks of *Die Kameel Kak* printed out on the back of her bank statements. Not only was she extremely wealthy, she was extremely frugal too. Maybe that's why she was so wealthy. At any rate, this lady wrote that since Doffie's passing, they had sorely missed reading *Die Kameel Kak* at their book club meetings, and would I mind please putting her on my list so that she could print them out and the book club ladies could continue reading about my antics in Egypt. I believe they thoroughly enjoyed reading them and for the next three or so years, I kept my promise and they received them each Sunday.

I cannot remember any of the ladies names, but if ever they pick up this book they might recognise some of the Egyptian stories.

Ladies, I hope you enjoy this book too. Perhaps it'll make your official book club list one day. If it does, it's all thanks to Doffska. M.H.D.S.R.I.P.

Red Wine, Amber Cognac and
a Double Shot of Golf

I met my bestest ever friend, Cynthia Daniels, while living in Cairo. Cynthia had just arrived and was stationed at the South African Embassy. The obligatory official welcoming party was thrown at the Ambassador's house and, as good, upstanding, citizens of the SA expat community, we were on the invitation list.

Sometimes, Peter would let Mohammed our driver have time off from driving us, especially if we were just scooting around Maadi. This particular evening, Peter drove the two blocks down from our house to the Ambassador's residence and dropped me at the front gate. As he was parking the Jeep, I barged up the driveway, wobbling in my high heels on the uneven paving, to meet the new arrivals.

"*Ahlan wa sahlen!*" I proudly greeted the newbies in my best Arabic accent. Cynthia looked at me a bit squiffy, but I could see the slight giggle she was trying to repress. I guess she was on good behaviour that night. I'm not sure I was though.

During the evening's festivities, and sitting in the beautiful gardens of the residence, enjoying the Spanish dance recital and the good food which Abdu the residence's chef had prepared, the Ambassador's wife comes up to me.

"Have you met Mrs Mbeki yet?" she asks.

Now I don't have one brain cell that stores political shit in my head, so I was neither impressed nor knowledgeable about who Mrs Mbeki was at that time.

"Nah," I said, taking another slug of the good red wine they were serving. Good South African red, to be exact.

"Well, come and meet her. She's our next President's wife."

I tipple across the lawn in my heels, slightly off kilter from the wine and find myself being introduced to an elderly lady with a warm smile in her eyes. She is wearing a traditional outfit, complete with a turban-like headdress as worn by Xhosa women.

There goes that devil again... he just can't leave my ear alone... and I feel the urge rising up inside of me. Before I can slap myself, I hear my own voice, loud and clear, saying, "How do you do Madam, Oh I love your *doek*! So beautiful! If I'd known you were going to be here this evening, I would have worn my own."

Bless her, she very magnanimously responded, "but you look so lovely too, my dear."

The Ambassador's wife grabbed me by the arm and returned me to my table, whereupon she instructed Cynthia, who was behaving herself admirably, to pour us all a very long drink.

Oh my, the good behaviour didn't last long. We soon found out that my new friend enjoyed red wine, cognac and golf. Not all at the same time. Mostly it was a good game of golf, then a bottle of red wine in the clubhouse then we'd end up with a jug or two of cognac while having curry at the Nile Bukhara. Until my fortieth birthday.

Ina and Allen had decided to host a small dinner in honour of my birthday and invited, amongst others, my darling friend Cynthia. We sat outside their villa enjoying the cool spring air of the late March evening. Eating little and drinking vast amounts of red wine finally saw me looking slightly squint. Again. Peter and Allen had made a secret pact that neither would drink that night. Us gals were blissfully unaware of this and continued to enjoy the constant stream of shots that the boys brought to the table.

The last straw was when Allen, fresh out of any more liqueurs for shots, starting pouring cognac into wine glasses. Cynthia and I enjoyed this tremendously for we both enjoyed a good Remy Martin every now and then. Ina, clever girl, had given up trying to keep up with us. She also knew she had kids to see to in the morning.

I hugged the palm tree on their front lawn that night even though I'm not really a tree-hugger. Cynthia sat on the *stoep* slugging back the cognac, saying how fine it was and it must have been a very good vintage.

I vaguely remember Peter seeing Cynthia to the steps of her apartment building, she was walking slightly off centre, balancing the wine glass, still filled with cognac in her one hand, and using the other hand to point her finger at the *boab* and shout at him for sleeping in the hallway. Which he did. Everynight. *Ya Pasha!*

Peter knows a good secret to preventing a bad hangover. What a pity he didn't teach it to Cynthia. He fed me two Panado's, a couple of Prohep and a Vitamin C with a glass of Coke. Then I threw up. Then I slept.

At 6am the next morning, when we were supposed to be getting up to go and play golf, both Cynthia (who was not answering her phone) and I didn't make it onto the first tee. I got out of bed around 9am, started baking bread and roasting chicken which our golf friend, Kelvin, thoroughly enjoyed for lunch after the game. Cynthia still wasn't answering her phone so she missed out on a great lunch.

She stayed off work for three days after that evening. To this day, she does not touch cognac, good vintage or not.

⁓

Cynthia was, and still is, the most steady-eddy straight down the centre golfer who never loses her cool and only occasionally loses a ball. I remember once playing with her in the first Egyptian Spring Open in Soma Bay and a *khamseen* desert storm had started blowing. Blowing is not the word. Howling is more like it. On a par three of less than 150 yards, every single person who teed-off used their drivers. And they didn't even make the edge of the green. That's how strong the wind was. It just pushed those balls right back at us.

So Cynthia took me to one side. She said "Patrisch, when it's breezy, take it easy." Well, what she should have said was take out your putter, you'll probably do so much better playing put-put than trying to hit shots up into the wind.

We came eighth overall in that tournament, just being beaten by Peter and another golfing buddy, Kelvin.

Kelvin worked for one of the hotels as their resident Engineer. He too played a mean game and got his Hole In One on a Par 4 at Katameya Golf Club just outside Cairo. Kelvin has now retired to somewhere back in the States and goes flat bottom boat bass fishing with his trusty pooch, Muttley.

So it was that when Cynthia put together the South African team for the Embassy Golf Tournament in 1998, she looked no further than to the three of us. Peter was immediately included in the team as his game was in particularly good shape those days. Allen, our Aussie rugby-viewing, cognac-pouring friend, by virtue of the fact he was married to a South African, and had lived in the country as a young boy, was asked to represent us. The fact that he played a mean game and could drive 275m with a five iron didn't hurt either. I, too was included, but only because there weren't eight good SA golfers in Egypt at the time and Cynthia had to make up numbers.

We decided to have a little *gees-vang* at our house a night or so before the tournament. It was a merry affair. I decorated the dining room with little South African flags. We had *boerewors* on the *braai* and Castle Lager flowing from the Coke fridge in the pantry. Cynthia and I were enjoying a good bottle of South African red.

As Captain, Cynthia had to dish out the golf shirts which I had embroidered with South African flags and each player's name over the heart. If there had been a prize for the best dressed team, we would have won hands down.

She also had to dish out the rules.

"Now then," she tapped a spoon against her glass to get everyone's attention. Ting, ting, ting. It took a while to settle the pack down. We'd really been enjoying the South African booze and were already halfway down a bottle of its finest *mampoer*.

Ting, ting, ting.

Sixteen pairs of eyes focussed somewhere towards the spot where she stood. We shut up. You don't mess with this *Tannie*. She started on the do's and don't's for the tournament, explaining the dress code. Then she ended with, "and I don't want any of you to use the P-word."

"What's the P-word?" someone shouted from the back of the lounge.

Putter! Pencil! Plugs! People shouted around the lounge.

"Poes!" Allen exclaimed in his finest Aussie accent. We all collapsed in a heap of laughter and giggles when Cynthia, our awesome Captain of such an unruly team, very sincerely and with an exceptionally straight face said,

"No, Andrew, P is for provisional."

CALICO CATS AND A DOG CALLED BEN

*D*on't get me wrong, I like dogs, but I don't like them living with me. They are smelly and they slobber and they leave landmines in your garden right in the path from the car door to the house. So when you're trying to lug all your groceries into the kitchen in one foul swoop, it truly becomes one foul poop.

I love cats. They poop in the neighbour's garden.

I've only ever had two pedigreed cats, the rest have been moggies adopted from the shelters.

"What's the name of your favourite composers?" Peter phoned me one afternoon.

"Mozart and Chopin," I answered, "why?"

"Which one would be black?" he asked.

"Mozart, why?" I have *no* idea why I thought Mozart was more likely to be of colour than Chopin.

"Come home and see."

Which of course piqued my curiosity to the point that I got in my car and went home, puzzled as could be. Welcoming me into my own home was the prettiest black kitten. I could see he had decided we were good people to have as parents. You know cats choose us, don't you? They just allow us to think we've chosen them.

His little sister was a calico cat, sporting orange, black and white in her coat. Here's another quick biology lesson. Did you know that calico cats are generally female? That's because colour in cats is a sex-linked trait. Girls have two X chromosomes, and with the colour orange being on the one X, they are able to display two colours plus white. It's rare to find boy calico's, but if you do find one, he will be sterile.

When moving to Egypt, we took them both with us, along with three Spaniels. Yes, I know I said I don't do dogs… but my husband does. So Baron, Tosca and Jethro were also packed up and sent north.

In our travels around the world, we always left with at least one less than we arrived with. Baron and Tosca went to doggy heaven in Egypt, Chopin arrived at the Kitty Pearly Gates in Kazakhstan and Jethro and Mozart both made it back to their place of birth before clocking out.

Peter phoned me as I was on my way home from work.

"Mozart's gone," he cried.

"Where to?"

"He died about five minutes ago," Peter was sobbing.

I put my foot down on the accelerator. As I walked in, my beautiful black boy who was nineteen years old, was lying in his usual afternoon sunny spot. On the patio in front of our house. His tail was waving gently in the afternoon breeze. A slight dribble puddled on the tiled floor below the chair. His body was limp.

As Peter was digging the grave under our Stinkwood tree, I wrapped him in a fleecy blanket, talking to him, telling him what joy and love he had brought to our lives and that we would remember him for eternity.

Mozart died on the 5th of December. The day Kacheturian was born.

"What's the name of your favourite composers?" Peter phoned me one afternoon.

"Mozart and Chopin," I answered, "why?"

"No man, other composers," he said exasperatedly.

"Ummm, Kacheturian and Poncielli?" I thought I knew where this was going.

"Which one would be black?" he asked.

"Kacheturian, why?"

"Come home and see."

Our black boy and white girl (aren't we the politically correct parents?) each have some of Mozart's traits. I believe he knew we couldn't live without him and so he gave himself back to us— twofold.

When I lived with Alma and Peter, we would congregate in their bedroom at night to watch TV. To prevent pressure sores, Peter would have to get out of his chair often, and so the most obvious place therefore was to have the TV where he could watch it too. From his bed.

Busty, Peter's dad, being a retired miner had taken to carpentry to keep himself occupied during his retirement. This made Carrie, his wife, incredibly happy. It kept him out of her hair and allowed her the freedom to continue with her bridge clubs and other interests. Busty made a three-layered tea trolley out of Rhodesian teak wood as a gift for my sister. This was used to bring in the dinners and tea when Pete was off his bum. It was quite a ritual, those evenings.

Dee Dee and I would settle at the bottom of the bed, on the carpeted floor, with eiderdowns and pillows. Alma would pour the tea from a large fat-bellied ceramic tea pot, straining the tea-leaves through a silver tea-strainer, inherited from our grandmother. One or two would always escape the strainer and I often ended up with a mouthful of black gunk which I'd either have to swallow or get up from my comfy position and spit out in the bathroom. I'd swallow. Peter would pour his tea into his saucer, blow it cold and slurp it down. The last saucerful would be placed on the floor for Ben, the Rottweiler to enjoy.

Most often after dinner, Pete would light a Texan plain cigarette with a wooden match from a yellow box of Lion matches. He would snap off the burnt head, toss it into the ashtray, and then pop that awful spitty-soggy match into his mouth, which he would chew on for ages. Then, when I was ready to go off to bed, I'd lean over to kiss him goodnight and he'd spit the match into my mouth. Eee-euw!

Another of his famous tricks on Miss Gullible here, was to have me sit next to him on the bed. Ben, the Rottweiler, would be lying at Pete's feet every now and then letting off a fart which would have us all waving our hands around and yelling, "phew! Piss off Ben, you smelly thing!" When Ben was well behaved, Pete would take my hand in his, playing with my fingers, massaging the inside of my palm. I adored Pete and so this display of his affection would just fill my fourteen year old heart with great beats of love.

Then Pete would manipulate my forefinger outwards while tucking the rest in towards my palm. Then he'd shove my finger up Ben's bum.

You think I was surprised? You should've seen Ben's face.

I can't tell you how many times I got suckered... each time thinking Peter couldn't possibly, wouldn't possibly do it again. Of course he would. And he'd laugh and laugh and I'd be mortified and embarrassed that I'd been caught out again.

But how I laugh about it now.

Blue Diamonds from Russia

The Kazakhs and Russians who worked for Peter, certainly knew how to put on a party. It was the middle of June, a hot and humid 40 degrees C and Peter's staff decided we had to host a summer party in the garden of our home. Now, this garden was large enough to accommodate five hundred people and in the centre was a swimming pool like I had never seen before.

Actually, I hadn't seen it until the spring thawed the snow. When we first arrived in Almaty, it was minus 22 degrees C, there was six feet of snow covering the yard and I had no intentions of traipsing through it at all. Lucky for me I didn't, for if I had walked across where the swimming pool was located, I would have fallen down 12 feet and probably ended up dying in a Trisch-made avalanche. And then Peter would have found my frozen body in the spring after being accused by the police of murdering me.

But just before Peter's ladies called for the summer party, I was in South Africa buying curtains for the house which we had just moved into in Almaty, Kazakhstan. I just could not find decent curtaining and finally used my frequent flyer miles to come back to Johannesburg with measurements for all one thousand square meters of home.

"You must buy a Creepy Crawly," Peter said over the line, "Go to Rivonia Produce and Hardware and get extra pipes too. They must measure at least 7 meters."

So I arrived in Almaty in the early hours of the morning on KLM's flight from Johannesburg via Amsterdam with two hundred kilograms of curtaining and 7.5 meters of Creepy Crawly piping.

Peter installed a pool pump and the Creepy, filled the pool with fresh water and turfed in the required amounts of salt, chlorine and acid. Our creepy was the hit of the party. While Jamilya Serkebaeva was entertaining the crowds with her talented violin playing, not to mention her very cute little body, curious spectators were standing at the side of the pool watching the Creepy do it sucking thing, up and down the walls of the pool. Kazakhstan had never seen a Creepy before. Generally they would fill a pool, swim in it till it was dirty, pull the plug to empty it and refill it again.

The Creepy fetched an unheard of sum on our departure from Kazakhstan. It probably is still the life of the party.

I also celebrated a fabulous birthday while living in Almaty. We had become good friends with a couple who ran the Hyatt Regency—our home away from home. Too often in winter, the electricity would go out at our house, and in minus 30 degrees C, there was no way I was staying in a house which would get cold in a heartbeat. So we would pack an overnight bag, phone Kostya, our driver and head down to the Hyatt where we would enjoy a warm bath, room service and a good night's sleep.

We had a dinner party to celebrate my birthday. Amelda,

wife of the GM of the Regency, was wearing a beautiful blue silk outfit. She was Serbian and had an amazing sense of dress. I admired the large blue ring on her finger.

"Is that an aquamarine?"

"I do believe it is," she answered, offering her hand for me to peer closer at the beauty.

The stone was massive and had a subtle turquoise colour. It was set in an antique silver setting, reminiscent of the days of the Russian Tzars. The double bands were the prettiest setting I had seen.

"Aquamarine is my birthstone," I remarked conversationally.

"Well, then," she said, pulling the ring off her finger, "I give it to you as a birthday present."

Despite trying to refuse her very generous gesture, she insisted on me taking the ring, saying that she had been in Tashkent, wandering through Gorky Park one evening and had purchased it from an Uzbek selling off his family's goods for five US Dollars.

"It's nothing," she said off-handedly, "I want you to have it. And when you wear it, you will remember me."

Years later I walked into the jewellery store in Sandton City. It was plush and jewels sparkled from bullet-proof glass-fronted cases.

"I'd like a quote on having this stone made into a pendant." I showed the salesman the ring. The size of the stone, I felt, was far too big on my skinny fingers and I had thought of changing it into a piece of jewellery I knew I would wear.

He called the jeweller over.

"Do you know what stone this is?" he enquired, reaching for his loupe which was hanging around his neck on a simple black cord.

"It's an aquamarine."

"Where did you get it?" He raised the ring up to his eye.

"It came from Uzbekistan. A friend of mine bought it there and gave it to me as a gift." I answered.

He turned the ring this way and that, peering intently at the stone. After a short while, he whispered, "Are you sure?"

"What do you mean, am I sure?" I whispered back at him.

"Well, for one, I don't think it is an aquamarine, and two, if it's what I think it is, you're not going to want to wear it in this country. Ever!"

The hairs on the back of my neck prickled. The energy in that little shop suddenly went up a good few volts. I almost felt the doors being locked and the alarm being activated.

"Have you ever heard of blue diamonds?" he asked in an almost reverent way.

Well I hadn't. And after he explained to me the only way he could certify that it truly was what he thought it was, I decided not to leave my ring with him.

Put it this way, if it isn't a blue diamond, then I haven't lost anything. If it is, I've lived the past ten years in comparative poverty to what I might have been able to live had I sold it—and even after sharing the spoils with the lovely lady in Almaty who gave me such an exquisite gift.

No Substitute for Black
Boots and Purple Hearts

I n the seventies, an all-girl band, Clout, shot to stardom with
their hit song 'Substitute', a revamp of the already well-
known Righteous Brothers song. Every radio station played it,
our fledgling TV stations aired the video, every disco DJ worth
his *dagga* stash had the single on his turntable at least twice a
session. And every 16 year old schoolboy had a wet dream about
one of the girls in the band.

My DH dreamt about Cindy Alter, the lead vocalist and
guitarist.

Now I'm no music boff, but I did know the song and I knew
the band who made it famous. I just didn't know the name of the
lead singer. So imagine the dim look on my face when I was asked
to interview Cindy Alter on a Friday morning community radio
show I presented.

"Cindy who?" I asked the producer.

"Alter," she said. Like I was supposed to know who *that* was.

"Ja? And that's who?"

167

"From the band Clout!" She was flabbergasted at my ignorance.

In walked a woman my own age. Except she looked about as young as I wish I could look. She was wearing a flowery top tucked into tiny denim shorts, with kickass cowboy boots. And legs to die for. She smelled of patchouli. Somewhere in the recesses of my other life's memories, I knew her.

"On Air in ten!" the producer yelled through my earphones. I hustled Cindy into a chair, shoved a microphone in her face, and started the show.

Cindy had returned to South Africa from the USA after surviving leukaemia. She and Stewart Irving, lead singer from the disco days of Ballyhoo had formed an acoustic band together. Alter Irving had just released their first CD. I played their version of Dolly Parton's 'Jolene' that day. We chatted and I played another track, and another and another. I could not believe that we had come to the end of the show.

I got home later that afternoon, still singing 'Jolene' and replaying my interview with Cindy.

"So," I ask Peter, "who do you think I interviewed today?"

Usually he would have listened in to my show and critiqued me, but for some reason that particular Friday, he had not tuned in. So he was unaware of who my guest had been.

"Who was your favourite wet dream when you were at school?" I asked him, almost bubbling with excitement.

"Cindy Alter," he said without hesitation. The man was breathing fast, probably thinking, if I get this one wrong I'm in the dog box for ever, never mind just tonight.

"Peter!" I say breathlessly after telling him about meeting her. "I really feel like I've just met my soul sister. I had this feeling that I knew her some time ago. We almost could read each other's minds and when she was relating her story to me, I felt like I'd gone through it with her. Does that sound crazy?"

The man who married me, nodded his head in agreement. He knows me, he does.

"Get yourself ready, my darling, we're going to meet her tonight."

Most often, Peter does not primp and preen for very long in front of the mirror, but that evening, he took extra care with gelling his hair just so, adding an extra dab of JPG for Men on his freshly-shaven face and pulling on a new shirt which he'd kept for 'a special occasion'.

Sitting listening to the acoustic excellence of Cindy and Stewart, Peter especially was in heaven. He had, as a young man, played some guitar and even sang the famous Clout song in a band he'd been in. His eyes were shining, his hands were clammy and I think he nearly died when Cindy gave him a fat wink. And when they joined us at the table for a light meal, I knew then that was the start of a very special relationship.

I'm quite shy when it comes to asking famous people to sign something for me. So when Cindy offered to sign my CD that night, I was totally over the moon.

The following day I eagerly opened the cover to read through the whodunit section of the CD, got to the photograph of Cindy and was blown right up over that moon and straight out of the universe when I read what she had written.

"To My Soul Sister, With Love and Light, Cindy xxx"

And she is.

GREEN EYED MONSTERS AND WHITE WINGED ANGELS

When my day comes and I arrive at the pearly gates and the guy with the silvery beard and flowing white garments puts his hand out and shouts "*Stop!*" I will probably look around and wonder who the hell he's talking to. Me? Can't be. Never. Are you sure? And at the nod of his head, I will puff up my already puffed up bosom, stomp my Jimmy Choo (oh, I wish) clad feet and shout at the top of my voice, "now listen here, Mister, this is just not on. I deserve my place in the angel choir. I have survived not one, but *two* mother-in-laws!"

What is it about mother-in-laws that they're mostly the bad guys, er, gals. From experience, I have vowed I will never do to my sons what my mother-in-laws did to theirs. Dislike their wives. For goodness sake, women, don't you understand it's you who brought up your sons to choose the women they want to spend their lives with? And if you truly love your boy unconditionally, surely you will love who he loves? Hmmmm, it's not that simple, is it?

My first mother-in-law was a simple woman who had the misfortune to marry a mean bastard. He was Scottish. He also dumped her for a younger woman. She never got over the heartbreak and carried a resentment and distrust of younger women who steal husbands to her grave.

Which is what I was. A younger woman. Although I didn't steal anyone's husband. He was fifteen years older than I and I have no doubt his sisters and his mother lectured the poor man on what trouble he was going to get into marrying such a young girl. I can just imagine the three of them wagging their fingers saying 'we told you so' when we got divorced five years later. Little do they know it was he who instigated the break-up.

"Happy Birthday, I want a divorce," was the greeting I got when I arrived home armed with a bunch of flowers, which, if truth be told, was given to me by my now darling husband. Truth be told, we weren't even dating at that stage, let alone having any of the fun stuff which would come our way shortly thereafter.

I was shocked. There was nothing I could say which led up to this divide except that perhaps, and I don't say this in jest, I grew up and he grew old. We didn't exactly have a bad marriage, we just didn't have a particularly good one either. In retrospect I think I was naïve to believe our union was happy. I thank him for finally giving me my life, which until that moment was on hold (even though I didn't realise it then) and freeing me from what surely would have been a dull and boring existence.

Thank you, thank you, thank you. For without that birthday greeting, I would never have grown and experienced this beautiful and wondrous life that I have been blessed with over the past twenty-some years.

My second mother-in-law was the matriarch of the family.

Although she is still alive as I write this book, she has become a very sad little old lady whose children bear the scars of her tyranny and who begrudge her the last bit of happiness she might ever have as her life draws to a close.

In respect of her status as the mother of my husband, we'll just leave it at that, shall we?

Black Balls of Pure Ecstasy

We were in Tashkent, Uzbekistan. Peter had invited his staff to dinner.

"We must go to the finest restaurant in town," he instructed his secretary, Irina.

I don't like Irina. She has legs that go right up past her armpits. She has a waist tinier than Barbie's. She wears cock-sucker boots and shorter-than-short mini's under her fur coats. And she's more than happy to 'settle' Peter in for the night at his hotel. When I'm not around, that is. Irina has also changed her hair colour from brunette (like Peter's predecessor's wife's hair colour) to silver platinum (like you guessed who's). She speaks little English and her typing skills are suspect. Peter does all his own Word and Excel documents anyway.

But Irina can arrange a good dinner at a restaurant which leaves me gobsmacked when I consider we're in a country where the average annual salary is less than what I paid for the coat I am wearing. And it's not an expensive one either.

Picture it. Walking up a curved grand staircase of marbled

treads with gold-leafed wrought-iron railings, I encounter two white-gloved attendants resplendent in full Russian regalia, one on either side of a set of heavy burgundy velvet curtains, edged with gold tassels. With a regal bow and a quiet swish, they part the curtains to reveal a dining room styled in pre-revolutionary elegance with antique chairs set around white-clothed tables, small lamps gracing the centre of each. Gilt-edged frames of oil paintings from some nobleman's mansion adorn the walls and in the centre of the vast ballroom is a floor of the most exquisite wooden parquet under an impressive domed ceiling. I feel like a modern-day Russian Tsarina.

Waiters appear from nowhere. They settle our party at the most prestigious location in the room and whip crisply starched white napkins onto our laps in one effortlessly choreographed movement. I notice that there is one waiter per guest. He stands just out of earshot, yet his eyes keep close watch without seeming to appear too prying.

"You must try the kazy," Mishka suggests. A platter of thinly sliced sausage meat is put down in the centre of the table. Glasses of vodka are poured from beautiful glass flacons. I put a morsel of the meat into my mouth and savour the unusual sweet smoky taste. Of horse meat.

Kazy is a traditional sausage made from the rib meat of a horse, stuffed into the horse's intestines and then either hung to dry or smoked. It is generally served boiled then cut into one inch slices, with rounds of onions and other seasonal vegetables as an accompaniment. And copious amounts of vodka. I can understand why. It's to mask the taste of the meat and make you so *vrot* you don't realise you just ate someone's pony.

The entertainment starts. A troupe of dancers enters the stage. They put on a spectacular display of traditional Russian dancing, the men demonstrating great strength and agility.

Their beautifully embroidered costumes incorporate the colour red. This colour is associated with beauty in Russian tradition. Their dancing is as attractive as their costumes. The women are exquisite; they have shapely legs and soft feminine arms and hands. They move effortlessly to the music.

The evening comes to an end, sadly, and it is time for Mishka to pay the bill. He is the company accountant and has brought an old faded brown leather messenger bag with him. The bill is brought to him for scrutiny. He adds up the columns, checking for accuracy and finally writes down a six figured amount.

"How much is that in US dollars, Mishka?" Peter asks. I can see he's panicking at the sight of such a large amount of Soum which Mishka is packing out of his leather bag onto the table. It looks like something you'd see in the movies for a large drug purchase. Piles and piles of notes are being stacked up in front of him.

"One hundred and five," he answers, "and that includes a very generous tip."

I can tell you that every time Peter visited Tashkent thereafter, and sometimes I would be with him, we would go to that restaurant to savour the beauty of dining in a traditional Russian dining room.

Not eating caviar in the former USSR is probably akin to not eating pizza in Italy, hot dogs at a baseball match or *boerewors* at a South African braai. It is an occasion to behold.

Caviar, the best of which comes from the icy waters of the Caspian Sea, is like eating liquid gold. The pop of each little egg on your tongue is just absolute pleasure. Eating caviar the Russian way, which in my opinion, is the only way, is the same as playing tag with the angels amongst the fluffy white clouds in heaven. Pure delight.

Dane and Justyn were home for the holidays. The electricity had once again taken leave of our home up in Gorny Gigant and we were, again, the guests of the Hyatt Regency. And when at the Hyatt Regency, we eat caviar. Not just *sommer* any old caviar you understand, not the red gooey baubles that come from salmon roe which you see in the supermarkets back home, but the real stuff which comes from the Acipenseriformes species (of wild sturgeon) in the Caspian Sea.

While caviar is exceptionally expensive when buying it at the duty-free at Schipol airport, in Almaty, it is quite affordable. It doesn't clear out your bank account in one foul swoop. Thank goodness. For this experience would be one that Peter, Dane and I would cherish for many years to come. Justyn, whose palate ranged from McDonalds to Pizza Hut and back to Kentucky Fried Chicken, had to settle for a steak.

Sitting in the white-cloth restaurant, and on our best behaviour, we eagerly anticipated our evenings treat.

The waiter sets down a bowl of ice shavings upon which are six small bowls bordering its edges, filled with chopped egg whites, egg yolks, spring onions, smetlana (soured cream), salmon slices and lemon wedges. Nestled in the peaked centre of the ice is a black tin, it's light blue and black lid proudly displaying for all to appreciate 'Beluga—High Quality Caspian Caviar.'

Picking up a buckwheat blini, I gently build a tasty morsel and set it delicately into my mouth. This is an affaire which must be savoured. The taste which I experience is like a nuclear explosion, building up across the soft palate and emerging through my nostrils with a soft 'pffft'.

I glance over at Peter. He too is in the throes of rapture. Dane, for once, has shut up, his mouth filled with the delicious delicacy. Justyn is happily munching his French fries and asking for more tomato sauce. *Pashalsta.*

Caviar comes from the virgin sturgeon,
The virgin sturgeon's a very fine fish,
The virgin sturgeon needs no urgin',
That's why caviar is my dish!

The Little Red Schoolhouse—Not!

I attended thirteen schools in twelve years of schooling. No, I wasn't expelled or thrown out of any, despite many of the teachers wishing they could have slapped me into space.

Daddy was a real rolling-stone. He gathered very little moss as we didn't spend much time in any of the towns we lived in. I'd just get settled into my new school, would have made at least one friend, caught up the previous terms' schoolwork and then the wooden tea-boxes and crates would be hauled out of the garage (which never housed a car, ever) and we'd be packing to move again.

My nursery school years were spent at Kettley's Country Day School. Miss Kettley had a small holding outside of Cape Town, near the air force base, where she ran a little school, catering for tiny babies and going up to 6 and 7 year olds in Sub B. I was dropped off there in the mornings and spent the day learning to do my three R's. Reading, Riting, Rithmatic. I particularly enjoyed 'riting' and still to this day people compliment my penmanship—when I have opportunity to use it. Sadly, since the advent of computers, and learning to type, I often find I can't write as neatly as I used to.

Lunch was served in Miss Kettley's farmhouse. No doubt it wasn't exactly large, but as a little child I was always in awe at going into the dining room and sitting down to have lunch with her. There must have been about thirty children, all seated at little tables, set with cutlery, napkins and salt and pepper shakers. Miss Kettley was the old colonial type. I still set my table as Miss Kettley taught us—with tablecloths, napkins and my 'best'. Well, what use is it to me when I'm gone—I'd rather have great use of it now, enjoying eating from Noritake and drinking from Baccarat, even if it is only to plate up spaghetti bolognaise and drink a Coca-Cola with it.

So at lunchtimes, we would wash our hands, sit quietly with them folded in front of us, our heads bowed, while Miss Kettley said grace. Then we'd get stuck into our food because, I remember, it was always delicious... and I was often very hungry too.

We moved to Namibia when I was 6 years old. I became enthralled with learning the metric system. Progress! My logical brain (some would doubt that) enjoyed working everything out in tens, hundreds and thousands. My math skills were far superior to my peers once I returned to South Africa. But, it never stayed that way, and I eventually had to re-write mathematics in Matric to get into University.

Namibia was still South West Africa in the days I lived there. I attended St. George's Anglican School where my best friend was Catherine, daughter of the Bishop of Damaraland. We would sneak into the church on Saturday afternoons to watch the Bishop marrying young people in the community, sighing over the bride's dresses and retinue colours. We'd have ballet shows with costumes from Catherine's Moms' studio out on the large verandah that went around the Bishops house, which was just up the road from the school. I still have a photograph of us, Catherine dressed in a medieval princess outfit, complete with cone-shaped head-dress of pink flowing chiffon, and me in a black ugly duckling outfit with a bright orange beak and black mask. Story of my life. Ugly duckling.

The Bishop confirmed my Mother in that church just shortly before he was deported from the country. I was devastated that my friend had to return to England. Was I ever going to see her again? Of course, we promised to write, faithfully, as friends always do. But the last I ever saw or heard from her was her crying and waving as they set off for the airport. Not entirely all her fault. My penmanship didn't stretch to pen pal letters.

And we didn't have email in those days.

I only survived my last 3 years of high school because of Lettie. She arrived in Welkom at the same time as I. It was the third term of the school year, friendships had already been formed, as had blossoming love affairs. The other school girls had already formed their cliques and none were going to crack slightly to let either of us in. To make matters worse, neither of us had school uniforms that first day of the school term and we stuck out like two very sore thumbs. We were the new girls. Our friendship was cemented that day in the fact that we were both outsiders.

I had been moved from an all-girls school where I was incredibly happy to a co-ed school with... of all things... boys! This was, ostensibly, so that I could be closer to my sister, Alma, and supposedly to have a more stable family life. Personally, I think I served a great charitable purpose - oh look, isn't that nice, she's looking after her baby sister, people would whisper as we walked through the town.

Anyway, Lettie had arrived from Rhodesia and was quite worldly wise. I thought she was fantastic and wanted to be just like her. I suspect I was looking for a role model and I found it in her. She spoke English like the queen, she knew how to French kiss and, pause here for dramatic effect please... she smoked.

We shared a lot in common, except I hadn't yet been kissed, and I most certainly did not smoke. I used to nick my sisters fags for Lettie, hiding them in my school blazer which ended up smelling like tobacco. We were both orphans in a sense. Lettie had been sent to live with her sister (who was a newly-wed and probably did not have any idea about how to look after a teenage girl) in an attempt to remove her from the dire situation her parents found themselves in as they battled to keep their farm in Rhodesia.

The country was going through a tumultuous change with young men dying to save their homes and farms. Robert Mugabe was inciting violence at that time, with the Rhodesian Bush War being fought by his Zimbabwe Liberation Struggle soldiers based over the border in Mozambique. No doubt Lettie's parents were trying to protect their youngest daughter by sending her to South Africa. Terrorist was a word I first heard through her and which filled me with dread and fear, especially when so many of the young men I knew at school went to the army, doing border duty up north. Some never returned alive.

Many of the boys at school took a great fancy to Lettie. She was buxom and shapely. Her beautiful blonde hair had life of its own, spending most of its time trying to escape from the yellow or blue ribbons the school forced her to wear. Most often, Lettie would buck the system by wearing blue in one pony tail and yellow in the other. And she had a certain savoire faire which had the boy's pubescent testosterone levels going up (as did other things they had). Lettie knew how to talk to the boys and they lapped after her like sick puppies. I, on the other hand, was freckled, skinny, had no boobs and blushed if a boy so much as looked my way. Which they only did when I rode into school on my little red Kawasaki.

See, at age 16, SA kids can only ride scooters and mopeds. We can't get automobile licenses until we're 18. So, while most of the boys at school had 50cc Hondas or Yamahas, I arrived on a beautiful shiny red 90cc which made them all lust after a ride on it, never on me, more's the pity.

Many an afternoon Lettie would ride pillion on the red bomber. Sans helmet, her blonde pigtails would fan out behind her as we darted down suburban streets to stay out of sight of the traffic police.

Tuesdays were my favourite afternoons. We bunked biology practical those days. Instead of dissecting frogs and peering at pieces of plant matter under microscopes, we would sit in the OK Bazaars coffee shop, Lettie smoking away ninety to the dozen. Not only would my blazer pong of tobacco from hoarding my sisters smokes in the inner pocket, but now it would take on a hum of its own from the constant second hand smoke of Lettie practising blowing smoke rings. Our biology teacher never once realized we were MIA for she herself took leave of the class and ensconced herself, with a nip of brandy and the latest National Geographic magazine, in the little back room off the biology lab for the duration of the practical session.

Of all the people I was at school with, Lettie is the only one I am still in touch with. She went off and married her sailor boy sweetheart, living her life in a small village where she is treasured by all who know her. My darling friend has aged over the last couple of years. Her youngest son died unexpectedly and, as I can only imagine, my friend's grief will last for eternity. As, I hope, will our friendship.

~

I was a great source of amusement for the boys in my science class. There were only three girls in the class and we sat up front at an experiment table on the right hand side of the room, right under the teacher's nose. While I was learning about bunsen burners, test tubes and conductive chemicals, the boys were sneaking into my bookbag left at the back of the lab, swiping my sandwiches and emptying my cool drink bottle which was always filled with my favourite crème-soda cordial. Then, at recess, I would find myself staring into an empty blue Tupperware box littered with bread crusts, crumbs and cheese wrappers and shaking the bottle to try and taste just one drop of the drink.

I believe in Devine Retribution. One fine summer's day I learnt about copper sulphate. I loved the turquoise colour it turned the water in the glass jar as we made crystals. My fascination with the vitriol blue popped the proverbial light bulb as I studied its toxicological effect. It became my best friend when I got a nasty shock after I sucked too hard on a pipette in the blue solution and got a taste of it. As did those awful boys the last day they ever snuck my lunch and cold drink. I took a teaspoon of the solution and popped it into my cold drink bottle. Shaken and stirred, the cocktail awaiting the main culprit was one I am sure he would never forget the taste of either.

I too, will never forget the colour his face went as he tried not to swallow the offending 'juice'. And it wasn't turquoise... oh no, it was a beautiful bright red. I swear I could almost see the heat fizzling right out of his *bok ore!*

~

Old Mrs Britz was quite possibly a fantastic piano teacher, but I don't know that I understood it as a teenager. She would hold a heavy wooden ruler with a steel strip inserted down the length of it just a couple of inches above my hands. If my arpeggios or scales were slightly off she would bring that ruler down with one *moerofa* crack, hitting my knuckles until they bled. Ok, that's an exaggeration, but I swear if I had one more slap on the hands in any given lesson than I had already received, my skin would have cracked and bled. For sure.

I would spend every afternoon straight after school sitting in her dining room at her very badly tuned and very stiff Yamaha upright piano which smelt of mothballs. As she opened the lid and removed the burgundy felt cloth covering the keys, I'd get a whiff of the naphthalene balls which were probably long gone, but the smell would linger on throughout Strauss' waltzes and Debussy's cake walks. Actually, I would have just preferred cake.

I think Mrs Britz gave up on me eventually. I was not a particularly good student and most afternoons I would make the same mistakes over and over.

"You go home now and practice this tonight," she would plead.

Of course I wouldn't. I'd sit down at the piano in the entrance hall of my sister's home, play one or two scales, check that my fingers were warm enough by cracking each knuckle and then I'd play Scott Joplin and Fats Waller, or I'd try to learn Ferrante and Teicher arrangements. I loved to perform, for sure, but I really found it tedious and boring to play Rachmaninoff instead of Rogers and Hammerstein. Who could hum to the Sabre Dance anyway? At least with R&H, one could sing about your favourite things.

Music has always been a large part of my life, but at school, I was all about singing. If there was a school concert, I was in the band. Usually as a backup singer. I never got the lead role. Instead, I was always the one at the back singing the harmony wishing I were a soloist on X-Factor.

In my second last year of school, however, I cracked the big time. Not only did I get to sing John Denver's Country Roads as part of a trio, but I also accompanied a young French Horn player performing "The Exodus". He could have exodussed me Frenchly anytime. Can't for the life of me remember his name, but he was cute... and he did have a horn... even if it was only French, and all French are poussays anyway, aren't they?

CLEAN WHITE SHITS AND
AZURE GREEK SEAS

Talking Greeks, I have had a wonderful affaire with the Greek community through my adult life. While I can't speak the lingo, I certainly can tell my *ghliko* from my *metreo* when it comes to Greek coffee. And the best is Pappagallo.

Peter and I met Dennis, our Greek God-Father when Peter was still working for Coca-Cola in South Africa. Despite his wealth, he was a gentle, kind and modest man. Except for his size which was directly proportionate to the amount of Greek feta, spanikopita and kleftiko made lovingly by his wife Rose and which he shoved in his mouth in absolute adoration of her culinary skills. Dennis was as wide as he was tall.

At age 15, he left his village in the Peloponnisos, Greece with just one small brown cardboard suitcase and the equivalent of a Grade 3 education. He could not speak English, yet he knew his fortune lay in wait for him in a country, the name of which he could hardly pronounce.

In the 1950's, artisans and labourers were eagerly accepted

into South Africa under an incentive programme. Dennis was ready to make his mark in the new world.

The plane landed at Jan Smuts airport. Dennis walked across the hot tarmac and entered the cool building. Inside was a bank of wooden counters, a Border Security staff member behind each one, ready with their rubber stamps and freshly inked blue inkpads.

"*Ja*, and what are you going to do here?" the customs officer asked him, lifting his eyes from Dennis' passport and giving him a *skeef* look.

"I am carpenter," Dennis lied with a straight face. He had been practicing those three English words for days, hoping that he wouldn't get the accent or the words wrong. Dennis was not a carpenter. The only thing he knew about wood was how to collect it in the hills of Skotchinoo in the middle of the Peloponnisos for Ya-Ya's outdoor wood burning stove.

"You got a job here already?" the officer questioned.

"Nê, yes," he nodded.

The officer raised his rubber stamp. It came down with a loud thud. Dennis felt as if his heart had just been kick-started again. He donned his hat, took his passport and quickly made his way through the doors. Once outside, he was greeted by a kinsman. Nick had come to SA years before and had a cafe in the suburbs. He was a friend of a friend of a friend of Dennis' father.

"*Yasoo! Yasus!*" he shouted in greeting, motioning for Dennis to hop into the two-tone blue and grey Ford Zephyr which was idling at the side of the road.

Dennis lived in the backroom of Nick's café for two years. During that time, he earned two pounds (or something) a month. Three quarters of his salary would be wired back to his family in Greece, some he would use to buy toiletries and the odd shirt or pair of socks when needed. The balance he would save to take over Nick's café one day.

Dennis not only bought that café, but also sold it to a very large corporation some years later, making a healthy profit. Around this time, he was approached by a Greek gentleman who stopped in at his café every evening to purchase milk, cigarettes and odds and ends which his wife had instructed him to pick up.

"I have a daughter," he told Dennis. "She needs a good husband. I think you will make a good one."

Dennis walked up to the house, straightened his tie, rubbed the toes of his shoes up against the back of his calves, removing some of the dust from the shiny leather. He had made the *mavros* spend the afternoon polishing them just right. He opened the gate and went in to meet his future fiancée.

His father-in-law-to-be instructed that unless Dennis had a house for his daughter, she would live at home for as long as needed. She was not marrying a man who could not keep her.

He hurried out the next day, purchasing a garden unit around the back of the café. They wed and, as they say, the rest is history.

⁓

Peter and I enjoyed a four week holiday to Greece when we were still young and gorgeous. We arrived in a swelteringly hot Athens one evening in August. Amidst the families waiting to greet other travellers, there we found Dennis, with a taxi driver in tow, waiting to take us under his wing and show us the best of Greece.

Drachma's were given to us, a couple of thousand at a time, by our darling God-Father. He took our US Dollars off us, along with a bank transfer note which we'd brought out of the country for him. In those days, South Africans could only take a set amount of money out on foreign trips per year. So, we were supposedly going to Greece on a business trip. That way, we could take the bank draft out legally.

My first topless sun-tanning session was on the beach of a Greek Island. Dennis and Peter were wallowing in the shallow, wave-less, azure waters, the salt calming Dennis' psoriasis outbreak. I was lying, front down, on a towel, my lily white body reflecting the suns' rays, reading a book I'd picked up at duty-free (when duty-free really was duty-free) at Jan Smuts. I was very shy and timid, not wanting to let on how prim I was, yet also not wanting anyone to think I was a slut either.

Out of the corner of my eye I noticed a little beige coloured car drive up onto the sand and stop about 20 metres in front of me. The door opened and a dirty, scaly toe-nailed, male foot set down on the white sand. I continued to read, but was now quite aware that I couldn't really turn over as I would expose myself to the person in the car. And then I saw what he was doing. Completely exposing himself to me, and with such a lewd grin on his sun-scarred wrinkled face too. All thoughts of composure went South. I jumped up, turned around and ran down to the sea, shouting, "there's a wanker, there's a wanker!"

Dennis and Peter laughed and spluttered, watching the man drive away as he realised I wasn't on my own.

Like I said, some old Greek men are no long Greek G-ds, they just became G-d-damned Greeks. Except of course for Dennis, who will be the best God-Father I will ever know.

We were having dinner at Dennis and Rose the evening before I left on another overseas holiday, this time without Peter. It was Christmas time, the most hectic part of his year, and he couldn't make the trip with me to the USA.

Rose had prepared our favourite chicken dish. Slow-roasted, with lemon, garlic and oregano which had been picked in the hills of Skotsinoo, dried in the barn outside Ya-Ya's house and then

Glad-wrapped into a parcel and sent back to South Africa in one of her sons' suitcases. Of course, at sixteen years old, he was stopped at the border post coming in to SA and had an hour's worth of explaining to do that it really wasn't grass, it was a herb. Rose also roasted big juicy red tomatoes stuffed with feta and mint. The side dish of potatoes were so crispy yet when you bit into one, you would find it soft and fluffy inside.

Sitting back, satiated, we talked about my upcoming trip.

"So, Trashy," Dennis said, "when you get to Athens, you take a taxi to the Platea Kala Yeron."

He was giving me directions on how to get to their penthouse in Athens where I had to drop off a suitcase. I was writing the instructions down phonetically, hoping to hell I wasn't going to *not* find the place and thus be saddled with said suitcase as I continued my journey onwards to America.

He handed me the key to the penthouse, explaining that the heating would be off and trying to put it on for a couple of hours wouldn't heat up the apartment quickly enough.

"Just sleep wrapped in blankets and you will be fine," he instructed. I knew how the cold in Athens in December could be miserable, especially as I was travelling from the thirty plus heat of Johannesburg. The idea of not being warm was uninviting. I even considered for a moment to stay in a hotel, but with the additional expense to an already tight budget, I figured I could handle just one night of cold.

"What's in the suitcase anyway, Dennis?" I asked.

"Pots and shits. Rothula, she buy new pots for thee kishen."

"Ok and shits? What are shits? You mean shirts?" I queried.

"Noh," he shook his head, "is shits for the bets."

"Dennis, I don't understand you. What is a shit? What is a bet?"

"Is the thinks you put on the thinks you sleep on." He said, quite exasperatedly, waving his porky arms around in the air.

Then the penny, which had been in the slot a while, suddenly dropped.

"Ah!" I exclaimed, "you mean sheets for the beds?"

"Ke-zacktly!" He clapped his hands, "new winter shits for the bets."

Orange I a Lucky Fish?

Now I'm a Piscean. A fish. We're supposed to love water. I don't. I hate the fucking stuff. I don't even spend a long time in the bath, preferring instead to shower. And quickly. I even think a swimming pool is a waste of good water, and it's a pain in the arse to keep it blue and clear and sparkling. For what? I don't swim.

I think I must have drowned in a past life. Probably I was the heroine on the Titanic with Leonardo di Caprio standing behind me, sailing forward into the winds, my hair flying straight back into his eyes and whipping them into tears. Oh hell, the violin strings just broke.

I've had two near-drowning experiences in this one life. If there's another one to be had, I'll probably just go with it.

"Look how I can jump in, Uncle Dick," I squeaked. It was an incredibly hot summer and I was spending it with my favourite aunt and uncle at their home in Roosevelt Park. It was the Christmas season, the fruit trees were laden with beautiful plump peaches and plums. I spent my days rotating between the trampoline, eating a piece of fruit, teasing the poor parrot, eating another piece of fruit, jumping on the trampoline and hitting the loo from eating all the fruit.

I was just about six years old and no doubt a source of great irritation to my older cousins. They were all a lot older than I. Lorraine already had her driver's license and she was the middle one. She zoomed around in a little dark green Mini. I loved going out with her. She spoilt me.

"I like these ones, Lolly!" I exclaimed at the little silver sandals.

"You must buy them for her, Mommy," the saleslady gushed at Lorraine.

Poor Lorraine. I don't remember ever calling her Lolly again after that.

So there we were, the whole family around Uncle Dick and Aunty Doreen's beautiful sparkly and clean swimming pool. I probably had bugged the bejesus out of my uncle with my constant requests for him to watch how I could jump in the pool.

I stood at the edge, squeaking and shouting at my cousins who were in the pool. I was wearing a little towelling poncho which my aunt had made for me. It was keeping the hot sun off my already sunburnt shoulders.

Unbeknownst to me, Uncle Dick had prepped the cuzzies, so, like a polo team they were well prepared to catch me. He snuck up behind me and gave a shove. I flew through the air and landed bum first in the water. As I sank the poncho opened up like a lily pad, and as I rose back up to the surface, it closed over my head like a morning glory at sunset.

It scared me shitless and I was convinced I had drowned.

Of course one of my robust boy cousins saved me, taking me to the side of the pool where I emerged from the water crying and hiccoughing and spluttering. Uncle Dick, in his stern way, probably felt a real heel for pushing me in as he kept saying "you're alive, aren't you? Stop crying for G-d's sake!" He also bought me a very nice present the next day. A set of roller skates.

I didn't swim again that summer. I think that was the birth of my realization that water and I just don't mix. Not even when stirred. Or shaken.

⁓

Which I was, quite shaken, nearly thirty years later after an adventure down the Zambezi River.

Peter and I were standing on the rocks way above the 'boiling pot'—the name the rafting company gave to the swirling waters underneath one of the waterfalls at the famous Victoria Falls in Zimbabwe. We were watching rafts filled with holiday makers and mad men setting off down the world's scariest rapids. It was Christmas day. With all our kids off at other parents, we had decided to take a four day break to Elephant Hills in Zimbabwe.

"C'mon Trischa, let's do that tomorrow," Peter urged, excitement shining through his eyes and burning into mine like a magnifying glass focussing a ray of sun on a piece of paper.

"Are you fucking crazy? I hate water! And it looks too dangerous anyway."

"No man, look. They have a guide so you just have to hang on, you don't even have to do anything yourself really." He argued, those eyes now creating smoke which clearly clouded my vision, for later that afternoon, I found myself signing on the dotted line, handing my passport over to some dude I didn't know from Martha, and putting my life into another *oke's* hands, er, oars.

I tentatively got into a raft on Boxing Day. Not being very religious, I covered my bases anyway by saying a quick prayer.

'G-d, please don't let me die today. Amen. Baruch Hashem.'

And then I did the watch wallet spectacles testicles thing. Just for good measure.

Our guide, I don't remember his name, but let's just call him 'arsehole' for short, was a young Australian who was seriously hungover from the previous days Christmas party. Hangover did I say? *Se voet*. He was still drunk. And everyone knows that drunk young Australian river raft guides are arseholes.

I should have listened to my gut. Get out the bloody raft... fast. Run away and don't look back as they head down the river and you head back to the hotel for a martini and movie in your suite.

Instead, I found myself backwarding down the river in the raft. Most of the time we weren't going forward, we were being shunted sideways, up and down, inside out, but mostly backwards while some Australian drunk waved his oars around shouting, "kawabunga dude!"

My first experience with a rapid was, to say the least, absolutely mind shatteringly scary. One minute I was hanging on to the raft which was still on top of the water. The next I was still hanging on, except that I was now doing downtime and I couldn't make out which way was up.

At the stage when I thought my lungs would burst if I didn't inhale oxygen without two hydrogen molecules attached to it, I let go. All 48kgs of me went down, baby, down. I opened my eyes (in panic I suspect... hell, I didn't need to know where I was going) and I saw white aerated water which I was convinced I could breathe. So I did. And I damn near drowned that day.

Popping up downstream, I heard the Aussie bastard shouting "grab the rope, Sheila!"

Spluttering in absolute indignation at being dumped in the Zambezi, I shot back at him "my name's not Sheila you *doos*."

Even in life-shattering situations I take umbrage at being referred to as a Sheila.

Nevertheless, I was hauled unceremoniously into the raft, given a fat *klap* on the back for having survived a grade three rapid, while everyone was laughing and joking and saying "check the look on her face!"

By lunchtime I had taken another dive into the depths of the Zambezi and I was not impressed. But, being the survivor I am, I decided to continue with the so-called 'trip of a lifetime'. I worried that it might become my 'trip to end a lifetime'.

"Oh don't worry, the crocs won't get you," said the oarsman with attitude, "the water's too fast flowing for any crocs to live here."

Yeah right. I'm going to believe you when you also said I wouldn't die in the rapids?

Peter, by this time, realised that I was not a happy chicken and so he climbed into the back of the raft with me. He hooked his hand through a strap at the back of my lifejacket and, with a solemn cross my heart kind of look on his face, he said to me, "If you fall out, I promise you I won't let go of you."

Three rapids from the last, our now seemingly sobered-up idiot of a guide shouted out, "you want to go left down the safe side, or straight into the devil's hole?"

That devil's hole dumped me down into its depths. I tumbled. I breathed in water again. I saw my children's faces go before my eyes. I saw my dead mother and father. I saw the white light NDE's (Near Death Experiencers) talk about. I heard the angels singing.

And in that moment, I shouted, "Not a damn am I dying today, G-d. I have far too much stuff I still want to do in my life!"

Well you know, the big guy upstairs has got a funny way

of giving in to me. He heard me loud and clear, but he said to himself, 'fine, she doesn't want to come here today, so let's really give her something to be grateful for.'

Well, Peter, as promised, had not let me go, and we popped up to the surface of the river. We were floating down between rapids, once again being thrown a lifeline from the raft.

"Peter, G-d have me three chances today. He's not giving me a fourth. I'm not going any further in this *verstunkende* thing."

The man understood. He didn't argue. He saw the writing on the wall. He instructed the guide to drop us off at the old exit point of the rafting adventure. One of the locals, who was guiding another raft that day, deflated it and popped his passengers across into the Aussies' one that we were vacating.

Pig. He didn't even give a backwards glance as he steered his wide-eyed passengers into the next rapid, shouting, "You're doing down today, you bastards!"

Five hours later, having climbed 150m out of the Zambezi gorge, traipsed through old landmine fields, walked through the border patrol wearing a really smelly t-shirt handed to us by an official (you're not allowed to cross from Zambia to Zimbabwe only wearing a swimming costume and a pair of strops) I collapsed onto the bed in our hotel room.

And, years later, when a friend of a friend of a friend said "hey, we're going river rafting on the Zambezi, you guys want to come with?"

I turned around, and smugly said, "been there, done that, got the t-shirt."

Jumping in with Two Feet and a Multi-coloured Umbrella

Why? What? When? Where? These were the questions Dael taught me.

Prior to going into business with her, I had pretty much accepted my lot in life. I was married to a man who had no desire to experience life, had no adventuresome streak in him, was happy being unhappy. I never questioned anything until I met Dael.

She is another of my soul-mates. I believe you can have more than one in your life. Each fills a space the other doesn't. Dael brought out the best (and sometimes the worst) in me. We loved and we fought passionately. With each other. And each time she said, 'why not? I would parry 'because.' And it drove her mad.

We would be driving down the highway and Dael would point out a billboard to me.

"Why does that advert work?" she'd ask.

My heart would skip a beat (not because my mitral valve was playing up again) but because any question from Dael would get me into a flat spin and a sweat. I wanted to be the good girl with her. Always. All the time. Until I found my mojo and could tell her to bugger off. I knew why it worked; why didn't she tell me what she thought instead.

Dael would do the same thing to me while I was designing on the computer. She'd stand over my shoulder and teach me about spacing and kerning, alignment and colour. I like to think I was a good student.

So there I was, sitting in the Rosebank Hotel coffee shop at 8am looking into the bespectacled eyes of a dynamic young woman in a navy-striped power suit, stockings and sensible medium heeled court shoes. She had an eagerness about her which didn't make her seem desperate. It ignited a flame in me which I hadn't felt before.

Dael had started a communications company and needed a partner. She had heard of me via some grapevine or the other and had called me to arrange a meeting. Her vision was enormous and I was smitten from day one. Little did I know that the path I walked with Dael would help to mould the business woman I was to become.

For years we worked hard. We grew our business and made good money. There was never anyone who could sell ice to an Eskimo in winter like Dael could. She sold our wares, I was the backroom girl, designing and invoicing, keeping the kids in the studio happy. Dael did road trips with our clients. I rode to the airport to deliver goods which had been left behind. Dael schmoozed. I snoozed. In my home office on the floor while the printers and cameras were running, my alarm clock waking me every two hours to change cartridges and film.

Then I got to go on a road show. What excitement! A large corporation had engaged us to do a huge audio-visual presentation and Dael needed me to help. The head of this corporation was a very staid banker-type-looking man. But he had an aura of power. And power always does it for me. He also said really nice things to me. And occasionally he sent me flowers (always as an excuse to say thank you for a job well done).

The presentation was over, the red wine flowed at the dinner tables. In my two-glass *poeg-eyed* haze, this man starting appealing to me. I was sex-starved in a lousy marriage and here was a man who wanted to bonk me sideways. I didn't argue. In fact, I almost pushed the man over the threshold of his suite.

Gentleman that he was, he saw me to the door of my room in the early hours of the morning. No *P.O.G.* allowed. I entered the room quietly, not putting on a light for fear I'd wake Dael up and have to answer to more of her questions. Unscrewing the toothpaste tube in the dark proved to be a bit of a problem too, but I managed to quietly brush my teeth and get into bed. I settled down, mentally patting myself on the back for getting to bed so quietly and not waking her up.

And then the door opened and Dael walked in.

We took our staff bridge swinging down at the Gouritz River. Of course we didn't tell them what we were up to. Instead, we just gave them instructions to pack a sleeping bag, warm clothing and a couple of bottles of wine. They went a step further and packed a bank bag of *dagga* too.

I heard giggling coming from the back garden.

"Whatcha up to?" I whispered, squinting through the darkness at the group standing in a circle on the lawn, just out of the square of light shining from the kitchen window.

"Shhh, she's coming!" One exclaimed.

"Put it out!" Begged another. Someone else giggled.

"Oh fuckit, Trisch, we're smoking a joint. Want some?" invited Grant, our only male artist in the studio.

I got a whiff of the sickly sweet smell of Durban Poison (or whatever they called it). Not having smoked *dagga* before, my initial good girl reaction was to put a mortified look onto my face, lay hand on breast and exclaim loudly, "oh no, I don't smoke that stuff!"

Then Dael pulled me into the circle, turned to Grant and said, "I'll hold her nose closed, you put it in her mouth, and then, you, Madam, suck!"

We both followed her instructions. Grant shoved the thing in my mouth. I nearly gagged. Then I sucked. Then I nearly threw up. I was thirty-three years old and I was breaking barriers and being a bad girl. Yay! I gained many Noddy Badges from my staff for my bad behaviour that night. And I vowed I would never touch the stuff again. And I haven't.

A sorry lot stood on the bridge of the Gouritz River the following morning. Dael peered over the edge of the bridge and remarked, "there's no way I'm doing that!" Not only did she do it once on her own, but as my partner, we did a tandem swing together too.

A young conservative Afrikaans couple walked onto the bridge. We got chatting to them. They told us they were on their way back from a Christian retreat where the Lord had given them a blessing to be engaged for marriage. They wanted to cement His word by putting their lives in His hands, in a completely figurative fashion of course, by leaping into a void and again being saved by Him.

Would we mind very much if they gave us their camera to take photos as they were in mid-jump and pendulum swing?

"With pleasure! We'd be delighted to help you document the last few days of your retreat!" we promised them solemnly.

As they were swinging their way into heavenly happiness, we were raising hell. Five of us lined up against the edge of the bridge, removed our tops, along with any underwear we might have been wearing, and finished off their 35mm film.

Clickety-click. How's that for a trick?

I can just imagine them asking the new mother-in-laws to pick up their photos at the Kodak shop. The mothers would surreptitiously sneak a peek at the photos in the pack, hoping to see prints of people praying together under baobab trees. Instead, they would find themselves viewing four by sixes of a bunch of young reprobates, four females with varying sizes and shapes of naked breast, and a guy with nipple rings showing v-signs to the camera.

And the old ladies would say, in horror, "this was supposed to be a Christian retreat they went on? *Vraggies! Nooit weer nie!*"

Twenty-two years later, my ex business partner is still one of my soul-mates. She lives in another country, far from me. She's a lousy communicator and I might get a message once in a blue moon on Facebook. I don't have her telephone number or her email address. Hell, I'm not even sure she lives in the county I think she lives in.

But when she flies into South Africa, she always contacts me. Then we meet for lunch or dinner and it's like we've never been apart. We pick-up exactly where we left off the last time. Like it was just yesterday.

ADD RECTANGLE PLINK
PLINK FILL MAGENTA

Once upon a time, in the days before CorelDraw, there was a graphics package called Zenographics. It was part of an autocad system which we used in our business to design 35mm slides. One had to be logical in the steps you took to create your masterpieces, for there was nothing like Edit Undo or Control X or Put To Back or Up a Level. Nope, if you put something in before you should have, there was no option but to press Delete and start all over again.

Grant taught me how to use Zeno. He was a whizz-kid, not only on the programme, but he was a fantastic artist too. Grant was going places with us. He would sit in the studio, cigarette in one hand, cup of coffee to the left of his keyboard, stylus in his right hand, and he'd plink plink, fill, add, plink, colour, plink, red for hours on end.

At the height of our success in the business, Grant left us. He packed up and went off to London where he became a designer for the SA Times. He spent hours meeting tight deadlines, he partied hard, got hooked on Speed, and met Andrew, who showed him the ways of the gay scene.

It was the early 1980's and young gay men were mostly staying firmly in the closet. Especially young gay South African men. *Dominees* and *Predikants* would try to exorcise the devil from a young man if they so much as suspected they were gay. Or they would excommunicate them from their church.

Grant's parents were staunch Catholics. When he returned to South Africa and told them of his love for another man, they refused to accept his lifestyle. Grant sank into a serious depression. He came back to work for us, but this time, we wanted him for good. We didn't want to lose him, so we offered him shares in a new venture which would focus solely on print media.

At our bridge-jumping weekend, we had asked the staff to bring small gifts for each other, signifying how they felt about their colleague.

"For example," I said, "if you think the person is really sweet, give them a packet of sugar."

Grant gave me handcuffs. He said it was because he never wanted to let me go.

He gave Dael plant bulbs. They were in an unmarked brown packet.

"That's because," he said, "you are always a surprise to me, so when these bulbs flower, they will be a surprise to you too."

Not too long after our Gouritz adventure, Grant walked into my office. He was ashen, he had tears in his eyes and his hands were shaking.

"I can't cope," he cried. "I just can't handle it any longer."

"What are you talking about?" I asked.

"Andrew's come from England and he won't leave me alone. My father won't speak to me. My mother prays for my soul. I'm tired. I'm scared I'll go back on drugs."

"Tell Andrew to bugger off, or I will tell him."

I'm quite pragmatic at times and often have no sensitivity to things which just seem iffy. Like Andrew. He was seriously iffy and I didn't like him one bit.

"But I can't concentrate on my work either!" he continued crying, "and I can't find a decent pic of a hyacinth for the flower catalogue I'm putting together."

I leaned over the desk and gave him a wad of tissues. He blew his nose.

"Oh man, Grant," I was exasperated at his depression, "just remember, this is your business as much as it's mine. Go back through the image library. There's got to be a pic of a hyacinth there. The sooner you get stuck in and finish the job, the more money you'll make, the easier it will be on you."

He got up, gave me a wry smile and walked out of my office.

That evening, Grant hanged himself.

For years I beat myself up, thinking, if only I'd listened to him, if only I'd known he was suicidal, if only I'd taken more time. If only.

Dael was in England when Grant died. Along with the staff, I attended Grant's funeral. It was a very sad time. I saw how devastated his mother and father were. We cried when his sister and brother recited a poem they had written for him. We sat in a pew at the back of the church, looking at a coffin which seemed far too staid for the young man we knew. If should have been graffiti'd or painted neon colours. That would have suited our Grant.

The organist started playing "Abide By Me." Suddenly the electricity went off and the organ's sound quavered to a halt. We got a fit of the giggles in that church when one of my artists turned around and said, "That's Grant. He pulled the plug. He'd rather they were playing Scatman."

Two months later, I walked into Dael's house. She pulled me by the arm.

"Come look here," she lead me through to the atrium.

In a beautiful pot, with sun shining down onto the blooms, their individual flowers making up a thick stalk, a fine fragrance filling the room, were white hyacinths.

She didn't need to tell me. Those were her flowers from Grant.

P-Parties Produce Purple Parrots, Pink Fairies and Puce Prostitutes

I never had the honour of being the birthday girl too often. In fact, I can remember only having three parties prior to turning thirty.

My sixth birthday was Red Indian themed and I was dressed in a Hiawatha outfit made from hessian which caused my pale skin to itch and come up in red welts. My sixteenth birthday was exactly that. Sweet sixteen. My brother-in-law, Peter, sat outside the front door, his over-and-under Smith and Wesson double-barrel shotgun laid across his lap and each young man walking through the door would get a *skeef* look and be asked, "Were you invited?" If he felt they were gate-crashing, they'd be sent back down the driveway with the gun sights firmly set on their rear ends. My twenty-first birthday was thrown by my sister, who invited all her friends. I got tired and went off to bed. Alone.

So, on the morning of my thirtieth, Peter, my beau, arrived at my office with a beautiful black forest cake and a bottle of champagne. He took me to lunch where we enjoyed another bottle of the finest. By 5pm, I was finished. We were sitting at the offices of a business associate where another bottle had been produced. By 7pm, I was not only seven sheets to the wind, but I was hungry too. Peter promised we'd go for dinner.

Driving on the highway, supposedly en-route to dinner, Peter suggested, "Let's quickly go home to fetch my video camera. I promised I'd give it to Bob for his trip to Zimbabwe."

"When's he going to Zim?" I asked wearily.

"In September." Now remember, I'm a Piscean so my birthday's at the beginning of the year.

"But why can't you give it to him in August then?" I asked again.

"No, he needs it now. He needs to learn how to use it," came the feeble response. Which I fell for, hook, line and proverbial sinker.

We drove into my townhouse complex. I got out of the car and in a rather miffed tone of voice, whined, "Well, if we're not going for dinner, I'm going to invite some of the people down to the pub for a drink to celebrate my birthday!"

"Great idea!" he exclaimed, "why don't you go across to the bar and I'll go fetch the gang?"

"Fine!" Now, as you all know, when a woman says 'fine!' best you beware. Nothing is fine. In fact, everything at that point in time is just *not* fine.

I stomped off across the driveway to the shared entertainment section of our townhouse complex. John was already there, playing bar-tender as he always did, wiping down the counter, making sure there was plenty of ice in the buckets and peanuts in old sundae glasses we'd nicked from the roadhouse down the road. Richard was sitting on his favourite bar stool. The TV in the corner was set to the local sports channel.

"It's my birthday. Hit me with a lemon drop!" I huffed and put my chin down on my crossed arms, looking at John from across the bar counter.

He poured a jigger of vodka then added a shot of Rose's lime cordial. I slung it back, pushed the glass across the counter and instructed, "Another one!"

May I pause a moment here. You're probably thinking that all I've ever done in my life is drink and be merry. Not true. I hardly ever touched booze until I met Peter. It's all his fault. I must admit though, that as I've got older I've certainly learnt to enjoy good red wines. I'm not keen on spirits, except for Southern Comfort and I love the taste of creamy liqueurs. Pity they don't like me too much. But being merry? Yes! I love being merry. Happiness is my drug of choice.

Recently, Peter and I decided to finish off all the little bits of left over liqueurs in our drinks cabinet. We had just enjoyed a good dinner and were in need of something sweet to finish it off. I SMS'd Dane with a photograph of some of the now empty bottles lining up next to the trash can. "A for Amarula, B for Baileys, C for Cognac!" His response? "D for *Dronk*".

Back to where I so rudely interrupted myself. As I am want to do.

So there I was, sitting feeling quite sorry for myself on my thirtieth birthday. The bar started filling up. People were slapping me on the back saying 'happy birthday you old fart'. Peter and Bob had the blasted camera on a tripod and were hooking up a light from the corner of the room.

"Stand just there for us, Trischa," Peter instructed, "we just want to do a test-run so Bob can see what the video will be like when he goes to Zim in September." They nudged and winked at each other, sniggering like two mischievous boys.

Clearly I was dense. So I stood in the corner, under the

spotlight as instructed, and continued to drink those wretched lemon drops. But then, as Frederich von Schiller, a German poet, quoted, "Every true genius is bound to be naive."

The lights dimmed. I looked around as everyone shouted "surprise!" Bob and Carol were carrying in a rather large, but very flat, chocolate cake, topped with so many lit birthday candles that I feared they might set the thatched roof of the pub on fire.

"Go on, Trisch, have a piece," someone shoved a slice of cake in my face.

Until I reached the age of forty, I didn't do sweet stuff. Chocolates could sit on my bedside table for six months, or until one of the kids nicked them. I didn't care for candy, biscuits or cakes. So I took the proffered plate and put it down on the bar counter. Little did I know, but that could well have been my first experience with *dagga*. The shits I called friends had baked a chocolate cake, laced with the green herb, hoping to see me stoned. Alas, I was more into the lemon drops that night. And the orang-u-tan.

I felt a tap on my shoulder. Looking around I was faced with a fierce looking gorilla standing behind me and singing "happy birthday to you" holding another bottle of champagne and erotically rubbing his belly (I think that's what it was) up and down my hip. The brute stripped down to a g-string, showing off a six-pack, tanned and oiled to perfection. I found myself being fed from this Adonis' beautiful hands, wishing for a bunch of grapes instead of its carbonated cousin. I was starting to feel champagned-out. Visions of white silk drapes, swaying in the breeze, ostrich feather fans keeping me cool, swept through my mind. I was hot, you understand. That's because my gorilla was absolutely gorgeous. The girls in the pub were whoop-whooping, egging him on, getting him to pour the champers over my body. I obliged, but with some trepidation, even in my blurry state. He was quite young and I kept asking him, "How old are you? Does your mother know what you're doing?"

That was the Wednesday night. Thursday most of the complex dwellers didn't make it to work. There were more cars in carports that one day than there would be collectively over a weekend.

We congregated in the pub again later that afternoon. To watch the previous night's movie which had been made by Bob and Peter. Yes, with the video camera which was so urgently required for Bob to take to Zim. You know, he never went there on holiday that September. But I did have a fabulous account of the best birthday I ever would have.

Saturday evening was my P-Party. It wasn't a T-party for Trisch, but a P-Party for my given name, Patricia. I had invited about one hundred guests to join me celebrating my thirtieth. They were asked to come dressed as something starting with the letter P.

My niece Dee, who is an amazing artist, was given the job of making a papier-mâché parrot head for me. She went twenty steps further by creating a set of wings and a beautiful tail from crepe-paper, reminiscent of a jungle Macaw's brilliant colours. These fitted around my arms, with the tail being secured to the back of my black leotard which I wore with black stockings and shiny high black stilleto's.

With the exception of one guest, who was in the final stages of pregnancy, and so came as herself, every person went to town, making sure that the P-Party would be such a success we would still talk about it for years to come.

Bob dressed himself as a prostitute. At over six foot, and skinny as can be, his fishnet stockings, leather mini-skirt and red lipstick made him a sight for sore eyes. He wore nothing underneath the mini. Carol, his wife, came dressed up, or rather, dressed down, as a Pensioner. Wearing *Stokies* over old brown socks, walking hunched over with a stick, a plastic leather-lookalike handbag swaying from her arm, with wrinkles painted on her face and her hair in curlers, she should have won the prize for best-dressed. If only I'd thought of it then. She'd also purchased a double G bra at Pep Stores for 99 cents and had filled it with Bob's hockey socks, which made her boobs hang down around her waist. Peter kept grabbing at them, but, can-man that he is, misjudged the waist-bound boobs and instead kept grabbing the real things.

There were Perverts and Pimps, Patients and Pilots, Poker Players, Primary School Pupils, Porters, Priests and more Prostitutes. I took my Parrot head off and left it on the bar for the evening. A couple days later, a friends' Mom said to me, "Michelle told me you looked lovely dressed up as a Petunia."

Pffffft.

ENTSCHULDIGEN BITTE,
YOU EAT GREEN FROGS?

The day we arrived in Switzerland, complete with one dog and a black cat, was beautiful. Sunny skies welcomed us to the house on the gold coast shores of Lake Zurich. We stood on the balcony off the dining room watching the rowers practising their strokes on the lake, lapping up the sun and enjoying the view.

Jethro, the idiot dog, was running around in circles. He was quite happy that he didn't have to go pee in the minus 30 degrees of Kazakhstan anymore where his piddle turned to icicles even before it left his body. Mozart was lying on the table preening and cleaning his already glossy coat looking for all the world as if he was completely at home amongst the mountains. Peter was reading the Lonely Planet Guide to Switzerland and I was opening cupboards and checking out the built-in steamer and pressure cooker in the kitchen. That's what us gals do. We head for kitchens and bathrooms when we move into new houses.

We were ecstatic that we were finally back in a first world country.

Then, the next day, the rain set in. For six miserable weeks.

We boarded the S1 train up to Zurich Hauptbahnhof. Peter was decked out in his usual corporate attire of suit and briefcase. I was wearing stockings and court shoes. It was his first day at the offices. Now, in all the previous countries we'd lived in, Peter had a driver at his beck and call. We were suddenly brought down to earth when the HR guy gave Peter train times and directions to the Head Office from the station. No driver. Bump.

At Zurich Hauptbahnhof, we changed trains to Dietlikon. Ten minutes later, we were standing on the station platform confusedly looking at the signboard which said Dietikon and wondering who'd stolen the 'L'. Back to the Hauptbahnhof we went on another train and tried again, except this time, while we got the name of the *dorp* right, we had inadvertently got on the express train and so went whizzing right past the station we were supposed to get off at.

What should have been a thirty minute train ride to Peter's new job took us over three hours.

Peter hated the trains. I loved them. I explored Switzerland on my Generale Abbonnement Pass, travelling to places with weird names like Hoch Ybrig and Pfaffenboden. I'd hop on a train early in the morning and bugger off down to visit my friend living in Geneva. She had been living in Egypt at the same time as us and we'd struck up a nice friendship. I'd be there in time for morning tea. She would give me a bag of *boerewors* to take home to Zurich. I'd present her with the *biltong* I'd made the week before.

Three weeks before leaving Switzerland to return to South Africa, the packers loaded up two forty foot containers of Rosema household goods. Mozart and Jethro had been shipped to South Africa already and were with Peter Green at his wonderful kennels in Pietermaritzburg, where they waited for us to arrive home.

We packed up the BMW and set off for Italy. Now let me tell you, Italy in mid-winter is miserable. Valentine's Day in Venice was so cold even the pigeons were puffed up against the wind and huddled in groups on top of the statues of St Marcus and co. We sat in a little restaurant warming up with *egte* pasta and a bottle of cheap, but good red wine. We visited the islands of Murano and Burano, zooting across the Venetian Lagoon on a tourist boat filled with other miserably cold souls. Even the furnaces at a Murano glass factory couldn't warm us up.

In Rome, we traipsed through the Vatican, where I sent Dane a postcard with a picture of his boss on it. Well, Dane worked for the Catholic Church in Rochester, NY, and the Pope was the head honcho of the company wasn't he? We threw coins in the Trevi fountains, we walked the streets of Rome, enjoying the bustle and the life force of the Italian city.

Moseying back up to Zurich, we stopped in Pisa where I truly wasn't as impressed with the leaning tower as I thought I might have been. Chances are it's because it was raining and the poor thing looked quite sad standing there all on its own with nobody to admire it. Except suckers like us. And we were getting wet.

We had just left Cannes and were on our way back up to Zurich when I noticed the petrol gauge in the car was nearing empty.

"You'd better fill up over there," I pointed to a gas station on the side of the road.

"Nah, I'll fill up at the next town," Peter replied.

It is sad, but true, that often he does this just to pip me off. He knows I'm nervous of being stranded at the side of a road with an empty fuel tank. I think it's a man-thing. When it comes to matters of petrol and cars, men don't listen to women. Sometimes they should.

The sun had set, the temperature had plummeted and we were driving up the side of a mountain. Our GPS system had given up the holy ghost and we were but a green blip in a mass of nothingness on its screen.

"I need to pee."

"You can go when we get to the next petrol station or I can stop here."

I peered out of the car. The narrow road was lined with tall trees, just a smidgeon of moonlight shining through their branches, creating a silver sheen to the icy tarred road. A fox ran out from the underbrush and scampered in front of our headlights. I had visions of it nipping my fanny as I squatted in the wild to take a piddle.

"I'll wait." I replied staunchly, my eyes still fastened on the fuel gauge which by now was sporting an amber warning light.

By the time my bladder was about to burst, we reached a stone-walled town at the top of the mountain and I heaved a sigh of relief. Until I read the sign showing that no cars were allowed in the village and also there were no petrol stations.

So off we went, this time, Peter was driving on Government Gas, freewheeling our way down the mountain. I was *knyping* quite seriously. Peter pulled to a halt, leaned over and heaved his laptop from the back seat to look up a map on Internet Explorer. Unfortunately, wherever we were, we had no 3G connection. We sat in silence for a while, both contemplating our next sentence.

I saw a set of lights moving towards us in the distance and jumped out, shouting hysterically, "help, help, please stop!"

A French-speaking lady with a couple of children in the back of her Peugeot station-wagon stopped. She spoke no English. Our French was non-existent. But we managed to get her to understand the lack of petrol scenario through unscrewing the cap at the side of the car, pointing in and saying *galas*. Which is actually Arabic slang for 'finished'.

She toddled off down the road. Well, thar she blows, we thought, but within five minutes, we were pouring a 2l Coke bottle of petrol into the tank from a generous old farmer she had found. Then, in very broken English, she said we should follow her. Which we did. Blindly, and with absolute trust. We had nothing to lose out there in the wilderness in the falling snow.

The town of Castellane, Gateway to the Verdon Gorge, was just two kilometres from where we had stopped. Unknowingly, we had been driving on the Napoleon Route through the French National Park.

We walked into the reception of a hotel situated on the edge of the small village square.

"Where can we get petrol?" Peter asked the man standing behind the desk. He was the epitome of a French mime. Black and white striped t-shirt and a black beret perched on top of his head. Sadly, he wasn't wearing white gloves and I almost took a step back when he answered.

"Ze gaz stashion iz clozed. Zey oh-pen at 9am tomorrow." His accent was perfect. Just as I imagined the French would speak our language. It reminded me of Clouseau in the Pink Panther.

"Derz yer dawg bahyt?"

"Noh!"

Grrr, munch, bite, snap!

"Ey thawt yer dawg derz nert bahyt?"

"That iz nert may dawg!"

Jean-Pierre (aren't all Frenchmen called Jean-Pierre?) invited us to stay in the hotel for the night. We were pleased to accept. We were hungry and cold. A good dinner, bottle of red and a nice bath would be in order.

"Dewyew vant viz or vizout show-err?" He asked us when booking us in, "iz fayve euro extra."

"Viz pleez!" I begged him. No communal showers and loo's for me thank you very much.

He showed us up a rickety staircase to a room in the rafters. It was reminiscent of Fawlty Towers. The shower was hot, the towels clean and fresh. Tra la la. The soap smelt of lavender.

We went back downstairs for dinner.

The dining room was quiet. Clearly all the back-packers (if there were any, it's really a summertime resort) had eaten and gone to bed. I did not hear any revelry from a near-by pub. There wasn't one.

Jean-Pierre was not only the receptionist, but the waiter and bar-tender too. He slapped down a huge cast iron pot of *coq au vin*, a delicious braised dish of chicken in red wine with morel and lardon. He brought a bottle of local Burgundy to the table, deftly uncorked it and poured two large glasses of the wine for our enjoyment. We tucked in.

Satiated, we dragged ourselves up the rickety staircase to our room in the rafters.

"I'm still cold," I said to Peter as I cuddled into his warmth.

"Well, get more blankets," he said, "I saw some in the cupboard."

I padded across the room and opened the old armoire to find a dozen blankets and quilts, crocheted rugs and throws piled up high. It was a treasure chest. I selected a couple and spread them over the bed, which was like a row boat. The mattress sloped down into the middle of the bed. Peter was hanging onto the one edge. If he didn't, he would have rolled over and squashed me.

I snuggled back into the bed, now covered with quilts and blankies which I swear were pre-World-War II.

"It was nine feet high, six feet wide, soft as a downy chick..." I started singing.

"Grandma's feather bed!" we both giggled as we settled down for the night.

As I said before, all French are poussez. Except for Jean-Pierre. I'm going back to his hotel one day.

So please explain to me. Why is it that every time we wanted to get out of Switzerland, we would end up somewhere in France?

At that time, you could check your luggage in at Zurich Airport a day before you were due to travel. So, being the intrepid travellers we were, we arrived at the Swissair terminal to drop off our luggage.

"I'm sorry, Sir," the lady at Counter 3 apologized, "you can only check your baggage in tomorrow."

"Why? Aren't you doing early check-ins anymore?" Peter queried.

"We are, Sir, but only 24 hours before your flight."

"But we're flying tomorrow," Peter started getting huffy.

"No, Sir," she politely interrupted, "your flight is only the following day."

We had read our tickets wrong. We had another day to spend in Switzerland. This wasn't a happy thing. We were both sick and tired of the anal shit the Swiss live in and which we had endured for two years.

Take for example the Cable TV and the Internet guys. Both had to come separately to our house to switch on their respective services. Both switches were next to each other in the box in our basement. Both guys, and both services, were from the same company.

Another example. I decided to go buy some ox-tail at the

butcher. I arrived on the dot at 12h30. They were closing their doors. Why? Because all companies and shops close for an hour and a half lunch. And that's it. You wait until two for them to open again. They also don't trade on Sundays. Which, in retrospect, isn't such a bad thing, it gives you family time. But to us *Farnies* who are used to having shops and movies and restaurants open seven days a week it's a pain in the butt.

Nou ja, so we left the Swissair terminal and trundled back to the hotel where we dumped our suitcases in the hotel room rather morosely, thinking about having to spend an extra twenty-four hours in the *verstunkende* place.

"What should we do now?" Peter asked. He was fresh out of ideas. And when Peter is fresh out of ideas he looks at *Kippie* here to come up with some type of fabulous entertainment for us.

"Let's go where the wind takes us, Bugs," I said, "let's get in the car and see where we end up."

So we did. And we ended up in some little French village across the Swiss border to the west of Zurich. To this day neither of us know the name of the village, nor the name of the restaurant we found ourselves seated at. Neither the waitrons nor any of the guests could speak English. Even the menu was in French only.

"Aha!" I cried, pointing to a dish on the menu, "frites! I know those are fries. Perhaps we should have that?"

"SMS Cynthia and ask her what the dishes are," my clever man suggested, "she can speak French, she'll know if it's nice."

So I furiously typed into my pink cell phone, 'we r sumwhere in France, want 2 eat. R animelles de moutons frites ok?"

The response came back, 'Lol! Don't touch. Bulls balls.' I wasn't sure if the Lol meant lots of love or laughing out loud. I suspect both. She is, after all, my absolute bestest friend.

"Jislaaik! Lucky we got Cynths, hey!" Peter sighed. For sure.

We ended up sneaking a peek at what other people were eating and ordering by pointing the dish out to the Maitre D. The French really are poussays. They all sat there so snooty, no doubt saying, 'the bloody English, they just can't stay away from us, didn't they learn anything from WWII?'

The good news is we drank lovely red wine and, because I was drowning my sorrows at not seeing Peter eat bulls balls, I got a bit *dronk*. Oy vey, again!

So it was that we finally drove into Switzerland at dusk. Our last evening in Zurich was awaiting us. Peter pulled up to the border post and wound down his window at the Official's hand gestures. We had learnt to greet in English otherwise we'd never understand them. Swiss-German is like no other language. It's all too sing-sing and fast for me.

"Greutzie mitternand. Passport please," the Border Post Official greeted us.

We both looked at each other, shocked. Our passports were in the safe back at our hotel. We had whizzed through the border post earlier and not been stopped. Neither of us had even thought about our passports at the time.

"Oy gevaldt!" I exclaimed. I slapped my hand against my forehead.

The official peered through Peter's window and said, "*entshuldigung bitte?*"

Now follow me on the phonetics here people and try to understand what I'm saying, for the poor fellow I don't think understood a word either.

"Wir sind Sud Afrikanischer."

"Aber Sie haben ein Auto in der Schweiz registriert," he queried, pointing to the Swiss registration plates on the hire car.

"I know, aber das ist ein ge-hired auto."

"Ja ok, und Passports?"

"Wir hat dieses passports and auslande auswiese in diese hotel safe gesluschen und forgetten."

"Warum?" he came back at me, steely blue eyes looking at my green and red-tinged squiffy ones.

"Wir hat ge-fedup geword with Zurich und wir hat in diese auto ge-klimmen en ge-bugger-offen nach France. Und wir are going zeruck nach Sud Afrika morgen und ich can nicht wag." And then I added, just in case my grammer was all wrong, "het het is."

"Ok, let me get this right," he said in perfect English, "you went to France without your passports which are locked in the safe in your Zurich hotel? And this is a hire car and you're going back to South Africa tomorrow?"

"Bezapt!" I exclaimed, clapping my hands.

The guy slapped his hand against his forehead and let us go.

I had just answered him in Arabic.

EARTH-TONED HUES AND A PINKLESS GNT

"Hey, buddy," our friend Jake exclaimed to Peter excitedly over the phone, "I just bought me an old Series 2 Landrover!"

"Whatcha wanna do that for?" Peter asked. This was an alien idea to the man who drove a roofless car with Pavarotti blaring from the speakers.

"Man, you 'n Trisch gotta come with us on the four by four weekend to the Free State. We're going in the Landy. I just put a fridge in it and we can pack some beers and a tent and we'll camp out for the weekend."

Did I mention the hotel thing before? Not only do I like to stay in hotels, but I insist on ones that have hairdryers and fluffy white towels, room service and TV's.

I did not do camping. I didn't even do caravanning, which I think is the same as camping, except you get to sleep with a roof made of steel and not canvas over your head. But you still have to use a communal loo and I refuse point blank to put my feet into a shower where I'm not sure the previous feet before mine have been.

But, after an evening of good food, great wine, camaraderie and coercion, I finally agreed to go on the suggested four by four weekend.

Now, let me warn you, Jake and Louella are not their real names. That's because we have had a lot of fun out of telling this story before that I really don't want to offend them by announcing who they are to the entire world. But it truly deserves a place in my memoir. It is an historic event in my life. So, this is written with tongue-in-cheek but more importantly with love for a couple who have been friends for as many years as Peter and I have been together.

Peter came home one afternoon with an easy-to-erect tent, a blow up mattress, complete with pump, and two sub-zero keep-the-cold-off-your-skinny-white-body sleeping bags in the boot of the car. He also delivered a couple of crates of soft-drinks in tins to Jake's house. Of vital significance was the tonic water he insisted Peter add to the stash of colddrinks. We would need this for the gins Jake had suggested we would drink while sitting around the campfire talking rubbish... like we usually did.

We eagerly awaited Friday morning for Jake to fetch us so that we could start our weekend away.

It took a while for us to get out of Johannesburg. It wasn't the traffic which got us stuck. We were at the licensing department for a couple of hours, waiting for Jake to get the Landy licensed before we could set off. No matter, we were in jovial spirits and so the delay didn't really bother us. Once we were on the road, the guys broke out the beers.

"Where are the Cokes, Jake?" I asked from my squatting position in the back. Louella and I were sitting on the camping gear. There was no back seat. Peter was in the front with Jake, the two of them clinking their beer bottles, shouting, "it's a boy! It's a girl!" depending of course on whether or not the beer foamed out of the bottle neck.

"Oh fuck, Trisch, I forgot to put them in!" He slapped a hand on his head.

"Jislaaik Jake, Peter brought you ten cases!" Louella and I shouted in unison.

"Ag, it's no problem," Peter remarked casually, "we'll get some at the next road stop."

By the time we got to the road stop I was parched. And when I'm thirsty or hungry, I get grumpy. But my spirits soon perked up once I'd refloated my boat. Back into the swing of things, we rolled out onto the highway, the Landrover giving a little wheeze at the load it was carrying. Watching the clouds ahead, Peter, the prophet of doom, glanced out of the window, stuck his finger up towards the heavens and declared, "I think it's going to rain."

No sooner had the words been said, the first drops fell onto the front windscreen. South African rainstorms, especially through the Free State, are generally preceded by great gusts of dust. So the few drops that had splattered in front of Jake's vision caused muddy streaks to run down the glass. He switched on the windscreen wipers. One worked. The other flew right off and disappeared into the grasses lining the side of the road.

Back on track after scrimmaging in the *donga's* for the elusive wiper blade, we laughed heartily and gave grateful thanks to the heavens above for having found it. It was fixed with a piece of wire nicked from the farmer's fence on the side of the road.

And then those heavens opened. They smiled down on us, said, thank you very much for saying thank you very much, now here, take this! We soon found out that Jake's newest prized possession was not water-proof. Frankly, we should have realized this when the wiper blade went sideways. Grabbing a pot, I stuck it on my head to catch the drips coming in from the leaky sun-roof. In retrospect, I can't remember if there actually was a sun-roof.

"Ag, it can't be that bad," Jake scowled at me through the review mirror, "you're making a mountain out of a molehill."

"You come sit here Jake and get the drip on your dome, then you'll understand. It's like the guy in Clockwork Orange when they drip-dripped water into his eye. Drives you bloody nuts, it does!"

We finally made it to the camp site, limping in and settling ourselves amongst the shiny new Discovery's, Range Rovers and Twin-Cab *bakkies*. The smoky smell of braai's were already filling the air, kids were running around playing tag, women were getting salads ready and the men were pouring hearty *brandewyn* and Cokes. *Eish. Ja, met ys.*

Peter started putting up our tent for the evening, Jake gibed "ja, you city slickers, you're a bunch of pansies with your fancy shit there hey! You just need an old army tent like mine then you'd have saved yourselves a fortune. What for, hey?"

"Aw, Jake, shuddup," Peter said during gasps of air as he *pomped* on the foot pedal to inflate the mattress, "we'll see who wakes up fresh as a daisy tomorrow."

"Ag, Pete, let's have a GnT, man. Hey, Trisch, bring us the gin, Louella, where'd you put the tonic water Pete brought us?"

"Eh?" She looked at him quizzically, "I didn't put it anywhere, you were supposed to fill the fridge at home."

"Ag, *bliksem!*" he exclaimed, slapping himself once again on the head, "I *blerrie* forgot to put the stuff in. Hey Pete? Ever had a gin without tonic? Gonna have one tonight, mate."

We settled into our tent. The campsite was quiet. Kids had been put to bed in their clothes, dirty feet and all. Men were *dronk vir driet*, snoring away, and the women were lying next to them happily thinking 'sjoe, lucky he doesn't want *nooky* now.'

Once again the heavens opened. I shot up in my sleeping bag, shook Peter and said, "what the hell's that noise?"

"It's just the rain against the tent, Trischa," he grumbled sleepily, "go back to sleep."

"But won't we get wet?"

"Uh-uh," he snorted, turning over, "we're in a cocoon here. Nothing's getting in through this sucker."

He was right. It rained all night and not once did I feel a drip. Not once did I get cold. Not once did I wake up again until the sunlight shone onto the top of the tent and created a blue halo around my head. I could hear the birds chirping outside. I could hear people unzipping their tents and putting kettles on to boil on gas burners.

"Hey Jake!" Peter shouted, "you guys making coffee?"

Silence.

"Hey Louella!" he tried again, "you got the kettle on yet?"

Silence.

We lay a little while, waiting for their response. Eventually Peter leaned over and unzipped the tent. He lifted the flap, and there, where Jake and Louella's tent should have been, was a pile of camouflaged army tent fabric under a puddle of water.

They had slept in the Landy with pots on their heads.

⁓

Now this same couple have been through many of our trials and tribulations, amongst which has been the referendum in South Africa, the turn of the Millenium including the Y2K bug, and the spot-on sights of a Hadeda.

The Hadeda is a rather large greyish coloured bird, part of the ibis family, which has an iridescent purple sheen over its wings. I love them. When they are startled or they are flying, they make a distinctive call which sounds like *ha-ha-haa!*

Hadeda's love big well fertilized gardens for they are primarily earthworm munchers. They enjoy Parktown Prawns - famous South African king crickets which are the ugliest things and just gives you the chills to look at. And Hardies also love other bits from the undergrowth such as insects, spiders and snails which they dig for with their long scimitar-like bills. Now that the biology lesson is over (Fannie would have been proud of me, despite bunking her practicals on Tuesday afternoons) Jake would tell you that the Hadeda, while it is mine, is not his favourite bird.

Jake, as you've probably correctly presumed already, is a gregarious fellow. He and I are two peas in a pod. WYSIWIG... What You See Is What You Get. His unreserved manner can sometimes offend people, but once they realise what a big heart he has, and his uncompromising loyalty to his friends, they want to, and often will have him, as a friend for life. Unless you piss him off. Like I said, pretty much like me.

One early summers evening, we were standing outside at our swimming pool, Peter was getting the *braai* ready and Jake, as per usual, was causing *kak*, giving Peter instructions on how to build a *braai*. As if he didn't know. He was offering this advice while slurping on his first beer of the evening, belching after a satisfied slug of the brew.

"Ha-ha-haa!" we heard the Hadeda's in the distance.

"Fuckers come 'n dig up my garden," said Peter, elbow deep in charcoal and fire-lighters.

"Ag, Peter, they aerate the soil," I defended the birds which also dumped half the soil into our swimming pool when cleaning their bills and having a drink of water after eating their fill from Chez Rosema's luscious garden.

"Ja, then they poop all over the swimming pool step," he continued, "and the garden service they won't clean it, will they?

Noooo, *kippie* here has to do it if Trischa wants to get in the pool for a swim."

"Ha-ha-haa!" the sound got closer.

"You better get out the way, girls," Jake said to Louella and I, "if they fly overhead they'll shit all down you and their crap is like a bubble gum machine gun. Fires all over the place."

The words had hardly left his mouth when a pair of Hadeda's flew over the garden wall. As they saw us, they flapped harder, changing their flight path right over our heads and with a *ha-ha-haa* and a sneaky wink at each other, they let go of their bowels. Both at the same time.

"Missed!" shouted Jake, raising his fist and spilling his beer as the pair continued flying up over the rooftop.

"Ha-ha-haa!" they winked at each other knowingly.

"Hahahahah!" Jake and Peter laughed, pointing at Louella, who was nearly ready to vomit. There, on the front of her freshly pressed, clean blue jeans was a splattering of Hadeda shit.

"*Jissis*, Lou, I can't take you anywhere," Jake laughed hard, pointing his finger at the offending mess, "look, they crapped all over you!"

"Wha-ha-ha-ha-ha!" I cried, pointing right back at him, "I wouldn't bite her so much shit, mister, talk for yourself."

And there, in multi-colored goop, running down Jake's back, was an artful arrangement of Hadeda Poop. In glorious hues of white and grey, interspersed with a smattering of yellow and green, smack bang between his shoulder blades.

Yellow and Brown, I nearly Drowned

While we're on the toilet humour roll, an incident in my youth has been a family joke for so many years that even my kids know it and enjoy telling people when we get onto the subject of city slickers versus country bumpkins.

I am a city slicker. Even as a kid I was a city slicker, despite running around barefoot and climbing trees. Which I did really well and from which vantage point I often stayed out of sight and couldn't be found by the other kids in the street when playing hide and seek.

But when I got to the farm, I really tried hard to be 'natural' at the country-living thing. There were no other kids to play with, other than Uncle Willem's labourer's children. They spoke a language I could not understand, and likewise, they were not familiar with English. So we generally pointed and nodded that we understood each other and ran around, playing in the fields and eating their mother's pot of *pap* which she would serve at 10am along with a spoonful of apricot jam.

I loved farm life. My aunt made her own butter which we

would spread lavishly onto freshly made bread every morning, her home-made marmalade and cheese shavings placed on top as an added extravagance. She was a stocky, feisty woman who could shoot the buttons off a robber's shirt at 100 yards. That's if he wasn't already running away, in which case he was likely to get one in the bum. Along with my mother, Aunty Gloria made up part of the Transvaal Women's Pistol Shooting Team. They were a formidable pair and I was in awe of my aunt. Truthfully? I was shit-scared of her.

Aunty Gloria started the first guava-roll factory in South Africa. The farmhands' wives worked in her factory which was just a couple of outbuildings behind the main sheds at the back of the farmhouse kitchen. The women would sit outside, in the shade of the Pride of Africa trees, their legs straight out, buckets to the side which would be filled with the peeled fruit, and they would sing softly together in three-part harmony. Inside, other women would add bags of sugar to the peeled fruit, mashing it down to a pulp. Then the mixture would be cooked slowly in huge pots, constantly being stirred so that it didn't catch at the bottom. Finally, under shade net, the conserve would be spread onto large wooden boards, covered in a heavy durable plastic and be left to dry before being cut, rolled and packaged for sale.

Another of my favourite activities was to jump onto the back of Uncle Willem's *bakkie* and ride with him into the farm lands while he checked on his avocado trees, sweet potato fields or ride across the river to feed the Drakensberger cattle which he bred. They were beautiful black beasts and I loved watching the little ones cavorting around the salt licks. At eight years old, I had the privilege of watching one of the cows give birth to a calf. They named her after me. I spent as much time as I could that holiday running after the little thing. Patricia lived for 12 years, producing many young. I don't think my Uncle Willem had the heart to knock her off.

Which brings me, finally, to my family's funniest home story.

Early mornings I would run up to the milking shed and watch in fascination as the farm hands filled up bucket after bucket of fresh milk. The cows didn't seem to mind these guys pulling down on their teats. They would munch happily at the sweet potatoes in the trough and once milked were quite reluctant to leave the shed. Often they'd get a flat slap on their rump with a push towards the door and yet they'd still try to nab another treat or two.

The milking shed stood proudly on the top of a gently sloped hill. It was a whitewashed building with a zinc roof, painted green. It housed a couple of stalls which could only be accessed by the animals from the opening at the left hand side of the building. A smaller door allowed pedestrian access on the opposite side. To the right was a wire fence running the length of the slope, under the branches of a row of tall eucalyptus trees, their scent a natural air-freshener for the constant smell of cow shit which permeated the area.

At the bottom of the slope were the cattle pens which Uncle Willem would use to treat his cattle for various diseases such as mastitis. It was there where he checked cows for pregnancies. It was also where he would drive his herd into the pens and shove them through a dip in the months when ticks and other pests or parasites were prevalent.

I think I was a dumb blonde even back then. I never realised why the farmhands, Uncle Willem, or my cousin Frank who worked on the farm (bless his soul, he was killed when a tractor turned over on top of him while he was trying to drive up the side of the farm dam), always walked along the wire fence to the right of the milking shed. There was a footpath carved into the red earth from many years of feet making their way up to the shed and back down to the dirt road. I just followed suit, walking up and down the side, against the fence, trying to be *au natural* and not the city slicker they all teased me about being.

"Pistrysie!" Uncle Willem shouted from the pens below. He had been testing his Drakensberger herd for pregnancies. I had watched with morbid fascination as my uncle stuck his whole arm up the beasts bum. *Eeeuw*, I'd thought, *eina*! And my attention had wandered to what the other kids were doing up at the sheds. Which is where I was when Uncle Willem called.

"Pistrysie!" he beckoned me down. "*Kom hierso kind.* Your aunty wants you to come to the house for breakfast."

"Coming Uncle Wil," I shouted to him from the doorway. My stomach was growling with hunger and I was looking forward to my aunt's famous bacon and egg breakfasts with stewed guavas, yogurt and freshly brewed *moer-koffie*.

Now, one thing you can't say about me is that I don't know how to get from A to B. I do. I have a fabulous sense of direction and my logical brain can calculate the most straightforward path as easy as 1-2-3. Unfortunately in this case, my brain forgot to take the report of pong from my olfactory senses into account. It also ignored the image of yellow and brown sludge with noxious fumes rising from it which my ocular senses were sending to my obviously befuddled brain.

I flung myself out of the milking shed doorway and computed, in my addled six year old way, that if I ran diagonally downward to the pens, I would halve the distance of the length and breadth it would take to reach my destination, making my descent down the slope more rapid and therefore quicker to get my little ass into Uncle Willem's *bakkie* which was heading to the farmhouse where my breakfast awaited me.

Problem.

I flung myself out of the milking shed doorway straight into the cesspool.

Neck deep I sank. Arms flailing, my skinny body feeling the coldness of the cow-crap in which I found myself sinking. Bile rising to my mouth as I realised what had happened, I started to cry. I was going to drown.

The farmhands laughed as they leaned out from the fence offering me sticks to grab onto so they could pull me to the side. The little kids ran from out of their hiding places to stand pointing their snotty little fingers at me, laughing while grabbing at their bellies.

Do you think Uncle Willem would let me ride on the back of his *bakkie* that day? Not a chance. He made me walk down the dirt road around the back of the house to the kitchen door, where my aunt instructed one of the maids to turn the hosepipe on me. Only once I was hosed down sufficiently was I was allowed inside, stripped of my clothing and plonked into a warm soapy bath. Feeling very sorry for myself, while everyone enjoyed the chortle, my stomach grumbled, reminding me of my farm breakfast now going cold.

And that is why, to this day, I am still a very proud city slicker.

Blue-Blooded Rhino's and White Lions

Did you know the colour of a rhino's blood is blue? It's not, but I figure it should be. They are regal and majestic animals who walk with an air of imperial prominence. They are noble and grand. And they are on the verge of distinction. And it is all our fault.

Living in Africa, I have taken for granted the fact that I can drive just a mere three hours from my home in the city and be in our national park, spotting the Big Five along with other wildlife which most folks only see on Nat Geo TV.

I have been up close and personal with a couple of rhinos in the Kruger National Park. We have walked with a guide to within one hundred meters of a huge old man resting under a tree. Peter and I have sat quietly at the edge of a dam, watching them drink the water at sunset and we have witnessed a herd of six of the biggest walk in front of our car, giving us the most splendid photo opportunity.

I am not a tree-hugger, per se, but I do take grave offence at little chinamen getting hard-on's because they take a *mootie* made from the horn of our beautiful rhino's. Already the black rhino has been declared extinct with extinction of the white rhino predicted in just ten years. What are we doing to our world?

I hope that my grandchildren, and yours, and our great grandchildren do not have to learn about the rhino through photos and videos. I hear you say "so what are you doing about it then?" And I point a finger right back at you too.

My first visit to the Kruger National Park was as a young kid. I did not enjoy it at all that time. I was shoved into the back of a VW combi and was told to keep quiet. My sister and cousin were probably peeved at having to take the snot-nosed brat with them as they set off on their safari. They were young and looking for wild animals. In more ways than one, I think. It was hot and dry and I couldn't see through the bush. I couldn't lie down on the seat either as there was a cooler box, filled with snacks and drinks, taking up most of the back bench. It was an awful day and I miserably promised myself I would never do this to my kids.

Which I didn't. Because I did not visit the Kruger again until I was well into my thirties. In hindsight, I could kick my own butt for I missed out on a wonderful way to enjoy life, being close to nature and just refreshing my soul out there in the bush. I have subsequently made up for that by enjoying every moment I get out in the bush.

On our return to South Africa in early 2003, we were invited to Tintswalo, a luxurious safari lodge in the Manyeleti Private Concession, its fenceless eastern boundary open to the Greater Kruger National Park.

Driving up through the Eastern Transvaal, I noticed the *veld* grass was burnt and there were white ashes in heaps dotted around the countryside.

"What's the white stuff?" I asked the group in the car.

"That's shit from the white rhino," said Andre who was driving. He looked at me through the rear view mirror.

"Really!" I exclaimed. "Why's it white?"

"Just told you, it's from the white rhino, that's why," He said with a straight face.

Gullible used to be my middle name... it stuck.

⌒

5am Sunday morning. The sun has not yet risen. There's an autumn chill in the air. The sounds of the veld coming to life can be heard, a bird call here, a monkey's chatter there.

Peter and I are the only guests awake. We walk quietly into the Main Lodge. The guides are in the lounge serving steaming filter coffee and home-made rusks, waiting to take us out on an early-morning game drive. They are a husband and wife team. She spots, he drives.

We wrap warm blankets around our legs. It's open on the back of the truck. A rifle lies across the windscreen, cocked and ready in case it is needed. Helen straps herself onto the spotter's seat at the front of the vehicle, hoists her gun over her shoulder and we set off.

"There's a lion and lioness mating in the reserve at the moment," Jan says to us.

We sit up eagerly, Peter with his Canon in hand, me with my video camera. These are our weapons. He shoots 35mm and digital, I shoot movies.

"Do you want to look for them?" Jan asks us.

"Yes please!" we both respond eagerly.

As we round a corner, Jan pulls the truck slightly off the road and stops quietly.

"Look!" he whispers, pointing at two o'clock.

In the early morning haze, we see a lion pair. The boy is

beautiful with a mane, thick and lavish. He stands to the side proudly, knowing that his mane is a sign of sexual prowess. The girl looks shagged. She's got scars on her body. There's a trickle of blood dripping down her neck. She snarls at him, gets up and walks a couple of paces towards him, presenting herself with a flick of her tail. Without a blink, he mounts her, biting into her neck with his teeth. She growls and slaps at him, her claws splayed out. He deftly avoids her swipes, then walks away, flopping into the dewy grass. She rolls over and lies quietly on her back for a few minutes.

"She's accepted his sperm," Jan says, "if it wasn't any good, she wouldn't roll over."

We followed the pair for a few hours. They put on a wonderful display for us, even mating out on the road. Lions can copulate thirty to forty times a day, for up to five days. The males' penis has spines which point backwards, and on withdrawal, it rakes the female's vagina, causing ovulation. No wonder the poor girl snarls at him.

"You have to come back in three months' time to see the babies," says Helen, "we are hoping to have a couple of white lions from those two as they are from up north in the Timbavati reserve."

She explained to us the genetic makeup of white lions, a recessive gene called the chinchilla mutation which was responsible for the colour. Contrary to popular belief, white lions are not albinos.

African legend has it that if a white lion is observed, it is an extremely good omen, sent by our forefathers as a sign of prosperity and well-being.

My white lion's name is Acinonyx.

He was just six weeks old when I met him. We fell in love and he sat quietly on my lap sucking my finger and dozing off to sleep in the warm Free State sun, making little snuffling noises.

Peter and I were guests of Riana, the founder of Cheetah Experience just outside of Bloemfontein. We had donated medicines for the animals and were being shown around their humble, yet extremely dedicated and loving sanctuary.

"Come look here," Riana said as she opened a side-door to a courtyard, "we don't usually bring visitors in here, but you're special, *kom kyk hier.*"

Inside the courtyard were two animals playing together. A pretty little caracul named Amy and a cute furry white lion cub with paws bigger than his body. He bounded up to me, squeaking and rubbing himself against my legs. I bent down and gathered him into my arms.

"His name is Acinonyx. He came here when he was 10 days old," Riana tells me, "he's a white lion."

I can feel my ancestors looking down on me and showering me with good fortune, prosperity and well-being.

A year later, Peter and I ride into the grounds of Cheetah Experience. We are on our way to ride Route 62 in the Cape on our Harleys.

No visit to Bloemfontein is complete unless we go to see Fiela and November, two of the many cheetahs there; Amy the caracul, Mischief and Shrek the leopards and of course, Acinonyx, my special friend.

He has been moved into a large enclosure with Jubatus, another white lion. There is a sturdy lapa built on stilts near the front of the fenced area. Acinonyx is lying on the deck, sunning himself. I call his name quietly and his ear twitches. I know he recognizes my voice. His mane is coming in and he is looking quite handsome. He's also started roaring, Riana tells me.

Lazily he moves position, allowing us to view his massive

paws which he crosses daintily one over the other. Then he yawns and we get a full frontal view of his strong jaws and impressive teeth. He looks straight at us and while lions don't purr, I swear I could hear one coming from him.

"He remembers you," Riana says.

Her words fill me up. I so wish I could hold him again, but I know I can't go into the enclosure.

He is, after all, a magnificent white lion, but still a wild one at that.

INTO THE WHITE LIGHT

"*L*ife is continuous, and is Infinite." - Edgar Cayce

I believe in reincarnation. I know I have been reincarnated. Hell, when you've been around the block as often as I have, you just know when you're back in the same old saddle. Déjà vu? No. It's something that sits so deep within your soul, you know its familiar refrain, you just don't remember all the chords.

How otherwise do I explain the day, when I was just a couple of years old, I turned to my parents and said, "When I was a little boy, I drank blood."

Oh sure, we can put that down to the over-imaginative visions of a kid high on ADD. Or perhaps I was that little boy, drinking blood somewhere? I've been known to enjoy the drippings of a rare roasted side of beef, scooping it up from the pan and slurping it with great enjoyment in *this* life.

Or what about when I was six, and we were driving over the Barrage near Parys in Dad's cream Valiant. We were, as usual, driving to see the family in Johannesburg for one or other of the holidays.

I sucked in my breath, "oh Mommy! I remember when we used to ride over that bridge and the water ran between the wagon wheels."

"No, my darling," my mother appeased me, "you weren't born yet when that bridge was built and it's never been open to traffic in your lifetime."

"But Mommy, I remember it! I remember when it was first just a little river and then they made it bigger when they built that bridge. I watched them putting in a pump."

I imagine my Mother and Father rolling their eyes at each other and quietly smiling at their daughter's over-active imagination. Or was it? The bridge I'm referring to was constructed over a furrow in the 1890's which fed water from the Vaal to Christiana as well as to the Parys agricultural region. Expansion and economic growth eventually dictated a more robust weir to be built, about one kilometre from the town, around 1910. At six years old I knew this?

And also, what about the time, as a twenty-two year old, I was taken to lunch at a restaurant housed in an old warehouse near the docks in Cape Town? I had just arrived at the airport and was being interviewed for a job (which I eventually accepted). Needing the bathroom, I excused myself from the table, climbed a set of stairs (the warehouse was below ground level), walked out the back, turned left at the edge of the building and found the original old 'outhouse' behind a shed marked 'Joe's Khaya'. All without asking for directions, and none being marked on the walls. And all without even thinking about where I was going?

I had not been back to Cape Town since leaving as a five-year old.

The piece of paper fell out of my bag as I reached into it on the passenger seat. I was driving in an area I was unfamiliar with and was scratching around trying to find my telephone book to phone the client I was going to see.

I read the name and phone number on the slip of paper, written in Wynter's handwriting.

"Mrs Brown is wonderful," she had enthused, "she gives such good readings."

I had only once been to see a medium and that was at a shopping centre in Johannesburg. Dael and I had paid her R200 each and she'd flipped a pack of old blue Bicycle cards, then, in an effected Russian accent and peering over them intently, had said, "Aye see very goot thinks in your fewtjure." It had not endured me to 'the other side' as I could have told myself these things and saved a couple of hundred bucks.

It was fortuitous having the car phone though, but still I dialled with trepidation.

"Ah, my dear, you are just two blocks from my house. Come and see me now." Mrs Brown said in a sing-song gentle voice.

I walked up the driveway of a compact face-brick house, it's paving flanked by standard rose bushes which were in full bloom. Pink petals opened to the glorious summer day and the fragrance which filled the air reminded me of the Vinolia soap my mother enjoyed using.

In the cool dining room, Mrs Brown sat down at the table and held my hand.

"I ask in the name of Jesus Christ, that the reading I give this young woman today is filled with love and light," she prayed. In front of her were a set of crystals, one white, one pink, one a blue so pure it took my breath away.

I kept dead quiet, my scepticism being held at bay. I wasn't about to give any acknowledgement that Mrs Brown was on the right path, so instead, I kept my eyes glued on the patterns in the white crocheted table cloth.

Only the hum of the deep freezer against the wall intruded on her reading. By the way, what is it that made the old ladies always put their deep freezers and pianos in their dining rooms?

The carriage clock on the dresser chimed three o'clock.

"There is a young man here," she said, pointing towards the ceiling. I looked up but saw no-one. What did I expect? A ghost of a guy hanging from the chandelier?

"He has a basket of flowers for you," she continued, "it's filled with white hyacinths. He says he found the photo."

I nearly had heart-failure. My darling Grant had been looking for a picture of a hyacinth for a catalogue we'd been putting together the day he had died. He hadn't forgotten me.

Suddenly, the other side seemed far too close. And I was close to tears.

"And there's an old man and woman here too. The woman has hair like this." She flicked her hand, gesturing a cow's-lick at the front of her forehead.

My mother had such a curl which she always sprayed heavily with Jane Seymour hairspray (the gold tin) to keep it from flopping down.

"The old man says to tell you your young son will pick up a pen and music will flow from it."

At that time, Dane was but six or seven years old. He had not yet started playing any instruments. We didn't even have a hint that he would become the professional musician he is today, having written concertos and suchlike which have been performed by international orchestras around the world.

I should have listened to my father.

When my day comes and I turn to walk through the tunnel towards that beautiful white light, I want to be able to look back on my life and say, "yes, I did it all."

I'd like to think that I've taken every opportunity presented to me. When I haven't taken it, I imagine it's because on some higher level I've known that it wasn't of any use to me.

I believe that when my number is called, I can go without hesitation, knowing that the lessons I had to learn have been learnt.

I want to look back and see every colour, prism and form that made up my personal Kaleidoscope shining from my earthly body. I want to enjoy the complex patterns of constantly changing colours and shapes which have formed my life for just a brief moment before facing the white light and walking towards it.

For then, in a myriad of colours, each individual piece falling perfectly into place, creating that masterpiece I call Me, I will have known, I lived a colourful life.

A colourful life which I have shared here with you.

-FIN-

South Africanisms and Trischerisms

Ag Nee Man - Oh No Man!

Ama-Bokke-Bokke - See Bokke / Bokkies.

Biltong - A South African delicacy, usually made from beef, but can also be made from game/venison. It is pickled and hung to dry. Eaten in various stages of being dried, such as wet and fatty (my favourite) or very dry. Similar to, but so different from, American Jerky.

Appelflap—A Dutch pastry similar to an apple turnover.

Bakkie—a pickup truck.

Bekam—how much?

Binnepoes-pienk -A hectic shade of pink. Usually a bright magenta.

Blerrie - Bladdy, bloddy as in 'that was a bloody fine shot old man!'

Bliksemed—to beat up, or to fall off, or to be very mad, as in *bliksem se donner.*

Bobotie - A Cape Malay dish, bobotie is spiced minced-meat with a curry flavour and an egg based topping. It is usually served with sambals and yellow rice with raisins.

Boerewors—a traditional South African sausage, usually *braaied* and eaten in a roll with mustard and tomato sauce.

Bok ore—Big ears which stick out so they look like a buck's ears.

Bokke / Bokkies - Our SA Rugby Team. Their insignia was the Springbok, hence the shortened version, bokkies or bokke.

Brandewyn—Brandy, but to say it SEfrikan way, it should be pronounced *brunne—vayhn.*

Brylcreem - An old hair-styling pomade for men. Before the days of metrosexual products like L'Oreal and Nivea.

Cherries - Slang for young pretty girls.

Dagga—cannabis, weed, dope. It is illegal to grow or possess dagga in South Africa.

Dankie—Thank you, thanks.

DD—Designated Driver. The one who abstains from drinking and has to watch all the others getting *dronk vir driet* and *poeg-eyed* and then has to drive them home.

Denningvleis - A delicious Cape Malay lamb stew flavoured with tamarind or lemon juice, bay leaves and spices to give an exciting sweet-sour flavour and lingering aroma usually made from fatty mutton.

DH—Darling Husband.

Doos—Derogatory term for a woman's vagina. Also used as a derogatory term when calling a man one... sometimes just means idiot.

Dominee—Same as *Predikant*. Preacher, Minister, usually of the Gereformeerde Kerk.

Donga—big furrows, ditches.

Dorp—small town.

Dronk vir driet - To be so drunk you don't come up from down. Typically when you're as drunk as this, you will end up crying. Sometimes from laughter, but mostly in such a distraught manner that those around you are the ones who laugh.

Egte—Real, original.

Eina—Ouch.

Erfed - Inherited.

Ertje Sop—A Dutch pea soup, usually so thick you can stand a spoon in it.

Farnies—nickname for South African Afrikaners (many males of whom have the name Fanie).

Fokof Polisie Kar - A local South African band.

Fooitog—almost like, oh shame.

Galabeya—A long tunic worn by Egyptians of both sexes. Usually cotton and shapeless.

Gat Gogga—Literally translated, bum bug, but mostly used as a form of endearment.

Gatvol—Sick and tired of. Fed up. Direct translation : arse full.

Gees-Vang - Literally to catch the ghost or the spirit. Usually an evening of revelry before going off on a Harley Rally. To get into the mood.

Ghliko—Greek coffee, sweet.

Haring—A Dutch Delicacy. Herring from the North Sea, usually eaten raw, sometimes pickled.

Ja - Yes

Jirre Got Gert—Jesus Christ, Gert, Gert being a man's name—and not that of either one the two *palooka's* frolicking in the snow.

Jislaaik—An expression. Like Geez!

Jou Ma Se Moer - Directly translated, "You Mother's ****". Sorry, but it's just too disgusting to write here... but I'm sure you get the drift!

Kaffir - An extremely politically incorrect way of referring to the ethnic people of South Africa and nowadays is completely taboo and actionable in court. It was used during the apartheid era as a derogatory way of oppressing people of colour.

Kak Bek - Literally means shit mouth. The cheapest red wine (in those days called Tassies) would leave a black stain around the mouth. So, when waking up the next day and feeling like every donkey on the Cape Flats had shat in your mouth, people would say you had Kak Bek.

Keh?—Slang for huh?

Kippie—little chicken. Usually used to refer to someone in a diminutive form of *Doos*.

Klap - Getting a klap is like having a backhander across the ears.

You duck when your Ma gives you a klap, but when she wants to give you a fat klap, you run like hell.

Koeksusters - A plaited dough twist, deep-fried in oil and then dunked in a sweet syrup, koeksusters are traditional treats, served with coffee at any occasion—christenings, funerals or just for **mos**.

Knyping—pinching, holding in.

Kvetching - Ok, not a South Africanism, but a Yiddish word meaning to... well... to kvetch!

Lekker - the Afrikaans word for nice, yum, tasty.

Lis—to feel like something, usually something to eat or drink. But you can also be **lis** to go to the bioscope.

Magies Vol, Oogies Toe—An Afrikaans saying, tummy full eyes closed. Usually we say this after a good Sunday afternoon roast, hinting we need a nap.

Mavros—South African Greeks refer to their black staff as *mavros*.

Mampoer—Moonshine! Makes you very, very *dronk vir driet* and *poeg-eyed* in a very, very short time.

Meneer—Mister.

Metrio—Greek coffee, medium-sweet.

Moer-koffie—Ground coffee granules which are boiled with water, making a strong brew.

Mootie—slang for medicine. Comes from the strange medicines prescribed by our local witch-doctors, the Sangoma's.

Morkels, Your Two Year Guarantee Store - A local furniture store, made famous by their byline.

Mos - Just for mos—just because. Just for the hell of it.

Na-dors - literally means after thirst. It's that hangover which requires a good glug of water or Coke to get rid of the shitty taste in your mouth.

Nogal - As well.

Nou Ja—Literally translated means no, yes. Used as a ho-hum.

Olliebollen—A traditional Dutch dough filled with raisins, fried in oil and then dusted with sugar powder. Usually eaten at New Year.

Oom—Uncle. Afrikaners call any man older than themselves Oom out of respect. They also call older women Tannie (Aunt). Any kid call me Tannie, I *moer* them.

Ossewa—Ox wagons. Used by the Boers during the Great Trek.

Padkos - Road food. South Africans put in sarmies, hard-boiled eggs, chocolates, sweets and cold drinks when they go on a road trip. Nowadays though we stop at the OneStops along the highway and buy Steers burgers and Wimpy Milkshakes.

Pap—a maize meal porridge, staple dish of the ethnic people of South Africa. Eaten with sugar and jam in the mornings, meat at lunchtimes, and again in the evenings. Whites get their maids to make *stywe pap* (stiff porridge) which is served with a tangy tomato and onion sauce, *boerewors* and chops at a *braai*.

Plaas –Farm.

Plakkies—Plastic sandals, thongs. In my youth you only got red ones or blue ones with little fish shapes stamped on the straps.

Poeg-Eyed - Squint eyed. Usually when one has drunk far too much and their eyes take on a life of their own, we say they are *poeg-eyed*. Sorta like *dronk vir driet*.

Poffertjes—A Dutch sweet treat. Little puffed pancakes, usually enjoyed with lots of powdered sugar and a cup of coffee.

Pomped—Pumped. Can be used as in you pumped the wheel up, or you had nookies with your girlfriend.

Predikant—Same as *Dominee*. Preacher, Minister, usually of the Gereformeerde Kerk.

Rigting Bedonnerd—Directionally challenged. Doesn't know up from down, right from left, this way from that.

Rookworst—A spicy pork sausage cut into slices in the *ertje sop*.

Skinner—To gossip. South African women love nothing more than a good *skinner* session about the bitch who lives down the road.

Skeef—Usually means to look skew or sideways at someone. But can also mean a man is gay.

Sommer—just because.

Sjoe—a sigh. Like 'shew!"

Stoep - Front porch, verandah.

Stokies—a pair of towelling slippers, usually to be found in Pep Stores all the way up to Woolworths. When going to hospital, men have to have their Stokies with them. Some old **Tannies** wear their **Stokies** out to the shops too.

Takkies - Sneakers, tennis-shoes but in South Africa, anything with a brand name like Reebok, Nike, Adidas, Sketchers is referred to as a takkie. Takkies can also be those black things you put on your car—the ones on your wheels… a.k.a tires!!

Tannie—see *Oom*.

Tikkie—just a touch of, a wee bit. Like *wit met a tikkie blou…* white with a touch of blue.

Verstunkende—the bloody thing.

Vraggies? Nooit! - Really? Never!

Vrek (cold) and Vrek (scared)—usually means you're so cold or you're so scared you're going to die.

Vrekking - Dying. In this case, the Dying Swan from Swan Lake.

Vrot—rotten.